Release the Dove
Workbook

By Rhonda Wilson-Dikoko

Table of Contents

Acknowledgements

This workbook came as an after-thought while editing my book. I realized that truly for people to understand how to take hold of the plow and break the necessary ground to obtain answers to their prayers and yes THE MIRACULOUS, I would have to supply some tools. You can tell now, I'm a proper farm girl. Because to plow the field and plant, you need seed, fertilizer, water and lots of stamina!

I am so grateful for all those who accepted to read this work-book and encouraged me to publish it. Notably Nicole Voelkel and Shola Bero. My "Dream Team" in The Netherlands comprised of Gail Matis, Helga E. Samuel and Bernadette Heaps was instrumental to the perfection of this project. Your tears, study of this material and the miracles that took place as a result of this study let me see the necessity of publishing this work-book.

My Pastors in the USA from The Double Portion Church, Pastor Hayse Moss and Sister Sarah Banks, you have upheld me over the years with your spiritual support, now I can finally walk! So thankful for you both!

To Reverend Amos Great and the The Ambassador's International Church of KL, You all are simply the best! Thank you for loving on my family and I.

I was so blessed to have Shereen & William Costley on my side of the court during Olivier's illness! They are beautiful inside and out! They were the most gracious and kind hosts we have ever had!

A thousand pounds of gratitude to my Gem Friend Carol Smart, to my Oasis leading ladies Barb Angell, Loma Steynberg & Susan Eshelman who were invaluable players in this fight.

My beautiful family are my biggest fans! Clement, Alesea, Mel, Obiale, Danielle, Olivier and Sanaa, my heart overflows and melts to know God has given you to me on loan for a season on planet earth! Let's make the best of it!

Love,

Rhonda Wilson-DIKOKO (aka KOKO)

Introduction

*T*he *ISV reads 'Consequently, faith results from listening, and listening results through the word of the Messiah'. Romans 10:17*

Throughout this entire ordeal (of my grandson's illness), my ears were quickened to hear the Holy Spirit. What was the Lord saying about Olivier's condition? When the doctors came for their visits, I would turn to the Lord to ask what He was saying. For me, the Word of God took precedence over what anyone else said. I realize this is a realm of faith where many do not tend to venture but I was completely ready. All preparations made prior brought me to the point of trusting Christ Alone.

I communicate a lot to the Father through prayer and also through songs. That's why there is a song selection inclusive in this work-book. You may google each song and use it during the week and or during your group sessions.

Many of these songs speak volumes to me and sometimes bring me to my knees. The first Sunday back at The Ambassador's International Church after Olivier's release from the hospital, the praise and worship's leader song selection seemed as if it were written for me. Every song and every word spoke to my heart.

Practice the habit of communing with God through songs. Whether you play them softly in the back-ground or sing them loudly in your car as I often do, let faith arise! If you go one step further to venture to see exactly why the song writer wrote a particular song, it is often from a place of brokeness. As if our God takes those tears, bottles them and shakes them around to pour out a sweet smelling fragrant perfume over His people.

The Word says 'Yet, you are holy, enthroned on the praises of Israel." Psalms 22:3. Another version says, He inhabits the praise of His people. But the scripture I really love is Zephaniah 3:17, 'The Lord your God is in your midst, a mighty one who will save; he will rejoice over you with gladness; he will quiet you by his love; he will exult over you with loud singing.' And that's what I believe the Lord did for me on that Sabbath day at Church, I could not stand but knelt in His presence. The Lord used Pastor Rhonny Fong to minister to me through songs, I was in awe of God's goodness. Bless you Pastor for being sensitive to the Spirit of God.

I wrote this work-book to accompany 'Release the Dove' because firstly, I was urged by my Oasis Bible Study women to do so but also I understood later from God it was His mandate and His timing for me as well.

The purpose of this work-book is to give you tools to live in the miraculous and get your prayers answered in a difficult situation yet being in a complete state of God given peace. I just spoke to someone who has been waiting on a prayer to be answered yet she is suffering from an anxiety attack. Dearly Beloved, that could have easily been me. I want each reader to be equipped to enter into each spiritual battle ready and prepared to obtain their God given promises. Always remember that according to the Bible, healing belongs to you when you are a child of God.

I did not include an answer key purposefully because I sincerely felt this was a study that needed to provoke you to seek answers from God's Word. Getting good marks is NOT the goal but retaining this Word and building faith are of utmost importance here.

Unfortuanately, this work-book cannot stand alone. It has been written exclusively as an accompaniement to 'Release the Dove Book.'

My suggested format for each session if you have a large group is :

- *This is a six weeks study*
- *Have name tags*
- *Have books and materials (paper, pens) ready for each member.*
- *Each member should sign the covenant page. By doing so, you promise you will not make your nail appointment a priority on Bible Study days! Prioritise the study always!*
- *Introduce one another via an ice-breaker making sure each new member feels welcomed.*
- *Leaders should pray over members and members should take time out to pray for one another. During our Oasis meetings, I loved having a prayer basket on the table whereby members could place their prayers anonomyously or with their names. I included these prayers in our recaps so that all members could participate in praying for one another.*
- *I encourage leaders to write out a schedule which serves as a visual that includes material to be covered during the week and the meeting dates.*
- *I admonish each member to do the homework to the best of their ability. This will help you grow in your faith. Also you will be ready for group discussion on Bible Study day. If you cannot for some reason do your homework, do not stay home but still attend the study.*
- *Please allow newcomers to have an extended grace period that never ends! Meaning a new person can even show up on the last day of the study!*
- *Follow up by recaps and also contacting members who are absent.*

Those are just a few guide-lines I included to help facilitate your study. If you are doing this study alone, you can still follow these guide-lines to some extent to keep yourself accountable.

Today marks almost a year to the date that I was sentenced to a Sabbactical by the Lord. My mandate was to complete this story. I began by doing Priscilla Shirer's study "Breathe". Then my story began to take shape. I wrote it in the form of a documentary because I wanted to capture every moment and every second of those dark days. I begin to write, edit and rewrite this story with much critical counsel. Then the search for a publisher and afterwards, one last glance by a writer and a final review by my editor.

Anyone who knows me well also know that I am usually a very busy person. Moving to the Netherlands was an opportune time to write as I had a blank page as well as a blank agenda. I knew it was God's timing because one year to the date of my Sabbactical I was offered a job! Loma Steynberg, I can almost see you giving me a smiley sticker with I DID IT on it! You warned me to take advantage of my Sabbactical and girl I did it, to my huge surprise and to the chagrin of my friends hearing, "I'm busy with my writing" at every invitation!

Please know that I wrote this study (and book) in partnership with the Holy Spirit. It is expressly the wisdom and flow of God that has enabled me to do so for your learning and for mine. Almost on every page there was a new insight or new information found. The researh was awesome!

My prayer is that you, dear reader, will benefit from my story. That you would not judge me from this content rather you would seek what is to be gleaned from these pages.

In His Service,

Rhonda Wilson-Dikoko (aka Koko)

Excerpt From *"Release the Dove"* Introduction

God collaborated with Pastor Moss in His prophetic Words----"Lord, bind this couple up tight, don't let anyone or anything separate them!"

It was a couple years later before Sarah would give me the photo and many years more before the Lord revealed to me our wedding covenant.

I don't believe either Sarah or I truly understood the signification of the photograph until the Spirit so generously revealed it to me.

The Lord first showed me the appearance of the rainbow after the flood in Genesis 9:1, **"I have set my rainbow in the clouds, and it will be the sign of the covenant between me and the earth."** *He promised he would never destroy mankind again by water. Whenever the rainbow appeared in the sky, it would serve as a token of a covenant between God and the human race! What a promise from a mighty God!*

I had left my family in the United States to follow my husband to the continent of Africa. This promise was relevant at all times as danger lurked on every side, yet God's covenant stood.

God revealed further our wedding covenant to me in Isaiah 54:10, **"Though the mountains be shaken and the hills be removed, yet my unfailing love for you will not be shaken nor my covenant of peace be removed says the Lord, who has compassion on you."**

Through our union, God would reach back to His promise in Genesis 9:13 and Isaiah 54:10 and extend these blessings to our posterity. Our eldest, Alesea would marry and produce her first son whom we named Olivier. His name was taken from the story of Noah who released the dove after the flood to bring back life the second time in the form of an olive branch (see Genesis 8:11). Olivier's name stems from the word olive and signifies life.

Rainbow
from
Heaven

Photo untouched

My hope is that as you read these faith filled pages, you will become one with God's Word and receive life! 'Release the Dove' has been written from a perspective of a desperate grandmother who would do all she could to preserve the life of her grand-son. It would take courage; it would take defying reality of what is seen and heard; it would take a stead-fast resolve and me reaching down to all I have learned over the years through my faith walk with the Lord.

It has been a journey with the protection of the rainbow covering my family with a covenant of peace. In all we experienced through this ordeal, we remained in perfect peace (Read Isaiah 26:3).

'Release the Dove' is a story of hope and abundant life. My prayer is that as each of my readers' explore this book; he or she will find faith to endure whatever trial you are going through. I release the Dove of Peace over each and every one of you in Jesus Mighty Name!

In His Service,

Rhonda Wilson-Dikoko (aka Koko)

<u>Instructions: How to Complete the Study</u>

Dearly Beloved,

I am thrilled you have come alongside me to study some very important principles found in my book, *"Release the Dove."* Though I ran a Women's Bible Study in Kuala Lumpur Malaysia for 6 years, it never occurred to me that I would actually be a Bible Study Writer! It was only through the prompting of the sisters from the study who upheld me in prayer through-out Olivier's illness that I was compelled to write his story. Only during the writing did I realize that for my sisters to truly grasp the spiritual concepts I was bringing forth, I would also need to write an accompanying study!

Thank you for joining me on this search for truth and divine healing! As I write, we just celebrated last week (October 2016), Olivier's winning a position as Class Representative. He had to convince his captive audience that he was the best student for the job! From the reports of the best Neurologists in South East Asia, this would not be possible so soon. Yet everything is possible to him that believes, Mark 9:23. Even BEFORE Olivier's illness, he would have NEVER had the guts to do some of the things he's done after his illness. This is testament that when God makes WHOLE, he does it Spirit Body and Soul!

Join me in this six weeks study and find out how you too can enter into the realm of the miraculous obtaining the promises of God for you and your family, loved ones, extended family, friends, neighbors..........all those in your sphere of influence.

As I customarily do with my Oasis Bible Study Ladies, I would like for you to enter into this six weeks covenant with me with an open mind. To promise to read and study diligently this material. If you are in a small group with others, you promise to keep confidential and within the confines of the group personal matters discussed during this study. To that end, write and sign your name below.

Name:

Signature & Date:

That's it dear Covenant partners! We are all set and ready to begin an adventure which I pray will enlighten each of your lives. I caution you to enter into this study with an open mind. All of what I say will be backed by scripture. It will be your choice whether or not to believe it!

Lastly, every miracle should be supported by indelible, irrefutable proof, several of the KL Oasis women saw my grand-son, some of you visited at the hospital. There are photos in the "Release the Dove" book attesting to his condition.

May the Lord God, open your spiritual eyes to His World of revelation and truth! May each and every one of you be blessed beyond measure as you study this material.

" [16] I do not cease to give thanks for you, remembering you in my prayers, [17] that the God of our Lord Jesus Christ, the Father of glory, may give you the Spirit of wisdom and of revelation in the knowledge of him, [18] having the eyes of your hearts enlightened, that you may know what is the

hope to which he has called you, what are the riches of his glorious inheritance in the saints, [19] and what is the immeasurable greatness of his power toward us who believe, according to the working of his great might [20] that he worked in Christ when he raised him from the dead and seated him at his right hand in the heavenly places, [21] far above all rule and authority and power and dominion, and above every name that is named, not only in this age but also in the one to come. " Ephesians 1:16-21

In His Service,

Rhonda Wilson-Dikoko (aka Koko)

Session 1: Covenant

Week One/ Day One

Covenant of Peace

Suggested Reading: Chapters 1-4 of Book '*Release the Dove*'

Let's begin this session by looking at the covenant of peace. On my wedding day, though I have no professional photo keepsakes, my sister Sarah with a simple Polaroid camera took this photo on page 5 which is untouched only enlarged. A magnificent rainbow was captured as we exited the Church walking towards our red sports car. After seven years of marriage the Lord revealed the specific meaning of my wedding covenant which transformed my thinking altogether! Thank God for revelation!

I felt the Holy Spirit instructing me to enlarge our photo which was still in its original size, put it in a special beautified frame, placing our covenant which he revealed to me, on the back inside of the frame.

In the 90's in Pointe Noire Congo, Africa this was no easy feat! Armed with my photo in hand, I walked into that small unique shop in the center of town. The owner was there when I explained what I wanted to accomplish in French, he looked at me intently glancing back down at the photo with a puzzled look on his face. I gave him no details of the miraculous sign on the photo, only instructions on enlargement. He needed a few days for this task when I returned he said to me using a strange expression, "*The devil was in the dark room with me, for the life of me, I can't enlarge your photograph*"! I would not take '*no*' for an answer. Tenacity is my middle name, encouraging him to try once more all the while keeping the original intact, he tried and this time a lovely 8 x 10 emerged with the rainbow showing in all of its splendor! It was now as if looking through a kaleidoscope I could clearly view every detail of color miraculously splashed across the page. Perched from my chair, I gazed at that photo with intensity and wonder of the majesty of our God!

The following scripture reads:

Isaiah 54:10, "Though the mountains be shaken and the hills be removed, yet my unfailing love for you will not be shaken nor my covenant of peace be removed says the Lord, who has compassion on you."

Do you think the sign of the rainbow on our wedding photo revealed to me later as a covenant of peace, extended to my children and grand-children? Why or why not?

_____

_____

What might the mountains and hills be referring to in a literal sense? _____

_____

Dearly beloved, scriptures are promises that are written for us and our situations in real time. Rephrase this verse/promise personalizing it to encompass you and your family. What are the mountains and hills in your life? Be sure to state them. _____

_____

_____

_____

Let's look at some background information on Covenant.

Reference: (http://www.biblestudytools.com/dictionary/covenant/)

The word "covenant," infrequently heard in conversation, is quite commonly used in legal, social (marriage), and religious and theological contexts.

The Idea of Covenant. The term "covenant" is of Latin origin (con venire), meaning a coming together. It presupposes two or more parties who come together to make a contract, agreeing on promises, stipulations, privileges, and responsibilities. In religious and theological circles there has not been agreement on precisely what is to be understood by the biblical term. It is used variously in biblical contexts. In political situations, it can be translated treaty; in a social setting, it means a lifelong friendship agreement; or it can refer to a marriage.

What is the origin of covenant? _____. What does it mean in two words? _____   _____.

The biblical words most often translated "covenant" are berit [tyir.B] in the Old Testament (appearing about 280 times) and diatheke [diaqhvkh] in the New Testament (at least 33 times). The origin of the Old Testament word has been debated; some have said it comes from a custom of eating together (Gen 26:30 ; 31:54); others have emphasized the idea of cutting an animal (an animal was cut in half [15:18]); still others have seen the ideas of perceiving or determining as root concepts. The preferred meaning of this Old Testament word is bond; a covenant refers to two or more parties bound together. This idea of bond will be explicated more fully.

What are the two biblical words most often translated covenant? _____

_____.

What is the Old Testament preferred meaning of covenant? _____

_____.

The generally accepted idea of binding or establishing a bond between two parties is supported by the use of the term berit [tyir.B]. When Abimelech and Isaac decided to settle their land dispute, they made a binding agreement, league, or covenant to live in peace. An oath confirmed it (Gen 26:26-31). Joshua and the Gibeonites bound themselves, by oath, to live in peace together (Joshua 9:15), although Yahweh commanded that Israel was not to bind themselves to the people living in the land of Canaan (Deut 7:2 ; Judges 2:2). Solomon and Hiram made a binding agreement to live and work in peace together (1 Kings 5:12). A friendship bond was sealed by oath between David and Jonathan (1 Samuel 20:3 1 Samuel 20:16-17). Marriage is a bond (covenant for life).

Choose one of the examples above of bonds in the Bible, read it and summarize what happened here. Share with your small group your findings. _____

_____

Marriage is a _____ for life.

Nuggets Gleaned from Today's Study:

+

+

+

Session 1: Covenant

Week One/ Day Two

The Heart of the Matter – How Covenant relates to me and you

Of a covenant between God and man; e.g. God covenanted with Noah, after the flood, that a like judgment should not be repeated. It is not precisely like a covenant between men, but was a promise or agreement by God. The principal covenants are the covenant of works --God promising to save and bless men on condition of perfect obedience --and the covenant of grace, or God's promise to save men on condition of their believing in Christ and receiving him as their Master and Savior. The first is called the Old Covenant, from which we name the first part of the Bible the Old Testament, the Latin rendering of the word covenant. The second is called the New Covenant, or New Testament.

Of a covenant between God and man; e.g. God covenanted with Noah after the flood that a like flood should not be repeated. Keeping this thought in mind, what do you think the covenant of the rainbow over our marriage consisted of? _____

_____

Now, how does this apply to you? If you are married or if you are single. _____

_____

Glance in your Bibles to Isaiah 54: 9-13. How did this covenant extend to my children? _____

_____

Look at this treasure of a verse!

"And as for me, this is my covenant with them," says the LORD: "My Spirit that is upon you, and my words that I have put in your mouth, shall not depart out of your mouth, or out of the mouth of your offspring, or out of the mouth of your children's offspring," says the LORD, "from this time forth and forevermore. Arise, shine for your light has come." Isaiah 59:21-22

Psalm 128:5-6 *"May the LORD continually bless you from Zion (Malaysia). May you see Jerusalem prosper as long as you live. May you <u>live to enjoy</u> your grand-children. May Israel (Rhonda) have peace!"*

How does the covenant of peace apply to my grand-son? _____

How does it apply to your children and grand-children? _____

Dear ones so loved by God! Isn't it just divine how this covenant of peace follows you wherever you go! For those of us who are expatriates, that's a blessing, isn't it? If this covenant of peace only is applicable to one location, things could get a little complicated. Thank God it isn't because at the rate we move around, I would have been doomed! Guess what, not only is it not related to just one location, nor is it related to one person! If you are a believer whether a rainbow appeared on your wedding photograph is of no consequence, you are under a covenant of peace!

That's news worthy of telling!

Now, let's see what you have learned about *Covenant.*

Please Match the Corresponding verses to the covenant by drawing a line.

The contracting parties were	Matthew 19:16 Matthew 19:17 ; Galatians 3:12).
The promise was "life" □	(a) God the moral Governor, and (b) Adam, a free moral agent, and representative of all his natural posterity (Romans 5:12-19).
Covenants of Works	The condition was perfect obedience to the law, the test in this case being abstaining from eating the fruit of the "tree of knowledge," etc.
The constitution under which Adam was placed at his creation. In this covenant,	The penalty was death (Genesis 2:16 Genesis 2:17).

This covenant is also called a covenant of nature, as made with man in his natural or unfallen state; a covenant of life, because "life" was the promise attached to obedience; and a legal covenant, because it demanded perfect obedience to the law.

The "tree of life" was the outward sign and seal of that life which was promised in the covenant, and hence it is usually called the seal of that covenant.

The "rainbow" is the outward sign and seal of my marriage covenant that includes my posterity.

This life covenant is abrogated under the gospel, inasmuch as Christ has fulfilled all its conditions on behalf of his people, and now offers salvation on the condition of faith. It is still in force, however, as it rests on the immutable justice of God, and is binding on all who have not fled to Christ and accepted his righteousness.

Session 1: Covenant

Week One/ Day Three

CONVENANT OF GRACE, the eternal plan of redemption entered into by the three persons of the Godhead, and carried out by them in its several parts. In it the Father represented the Godhead in its indivisible sovereignty, and the Son his people as their surety (John 17:4 John 17:6 John 17:9 ; Isaiah 42:6 ; Psalms 89:3).

After this reading. Please discuss the signification of the Covenant of Grace vs Works. Write your observations here:

1-

2-

3-

4-

5-*From what you understand about covenant, how would my belief in the covenant of peace affect my stance during Olivier's illness?*

_____

_____

6 - Now that you realize as a believer, the covenant of peace belongs to you and your family, how does this change your outlook on ongoing issues you might be experiencing in your life and extended family at the moment? _____

_____

How does this knowledge of the covenant of peace provide a different viewpoint? _____

_____

Looking through your spiritual binoculars towards the future, Read Jeremiah 29:11 or Romans 8:28 for further proof. Share your ideas here.

_____

_____

_____

_____

Please take your time and study the accompanying verses of the above previous reading regarding Covenant. Use this space to take notes.

Session 1: Covenant

Week One/ Day Four

The Covenant of Salvation

Your stand with Christ and the question of salvation is more important than healing, more important than finances and soundness of mind! More important than your husband or wife, family or children. The question of salvation must be answered while you are still living and on this earth according to God's Word.

I was saddened to hear a very important Chaplain in the USA say in the horrific aftermath of the 911 occurrence that the lives of the souls of the Fire Fighters are surely in heaven because they were doing God's work in saving people's lives.

Clearly the Bible has shown us that it is not through works that we are saved.

Ephesians 2: 8-10: *"For it is by grace you have been saved, through faith—and this is not from yourselves, it is the gift of God— 9 not by works, so that no one can boast. 10 For we are God's handiwork, created in Christ Jesus to do good works, which God prepared in advance for us to do."*

So though we were all touched by the selfless service of the Firefighters and indeed others during the Terrorists attacks in September of 2001, their acts do not guarantee eternal life. Only their stance with Christ.

When people die and especially in the aftermath of such great destruction in our nation (USA), it is difficult to get the formula right. But as scholars of the Bible, we must be accurate to our listeners for their lives might depend upon what we say or do not say.

I had an interesting conversation with my neighbor about salvation in Dutch over Sunday brunch last week. The entire exchange took place in Dutch and though I groped and searched for a simple way to explain eternity and salvation to him his response was similar to that of a native **English Speaker!** Salvation to him involved works and whether you were good or bad. So basically the Old Covenant which is _____. I pointed out to him the same verses mentioned above but from my Dutch Bible in Ephesians 2:8-9.

For fun, if your language is not English, find Ephesians 2:8-9 and write it out in your language or any other language you know. If your language is English, then write it in Dutch! In this way, you get to learn Dutch with me. I daresay, our SA friends have the upper hand as Afrikaans is similar!

_____

My neighbor wondered about all the bad people in the world. I told him salvation was personal, and for the moment, I was only concerned about him! On that note, he politely excused himself to join his wife downstairs. Who are the ones in your life whom you are concerned over for their salvation? Say a silent prayer for them now.

17

This exchange took place the same week I had been involved in a break out group that took evangelization to the streets of The Hague. My daughter Danielle was my partner. We were commissioned out in twos! Armed with a Bible in Chinese and one in English, brochures on Salvation and Business cards from our Church, we hit the streets!

Initially, we weren't well received at all! Arriving at the Central Station, I met a gentleman who barely spoke English. So between my struggling Dutch and his broken English, we established that he was already a Christian and he proceeded to show me his cross! We continued with a few more pleasantries before my partner and I stepped back outside into the rainy cold night. Just near the door, I spotted an elderly gentleman and walked up to him. He looked lost and dejected and began to cry. He too only spoke Dutch. He pointed to his back to indicate he was in a lot of pain. I offered to pray for him and he accepted. In the end, he gave me a thumbs up and said in English, '*Jesus is the best*!'

So important is the message of salvation that we need boldness to speak to our family members, neighbors and people on the streets. We need to become radical in our approach to salvation for others. My friend Jackie sends me faithfully daily devotionals from *Woodedge Community*. Yesterday she sent me one entitled: Immortal Souls. Here is an excerpt:

> One more example of the power of praying for lost people. David Brainerd was a missionary to Indians in New England in Colonial America. He fell in love with the daughter of Jonathan Edwards, the great pastor and theologian in Colonial America. However he died of tuberculosis before they married, at the age of 29.
>
> Brainerd's impact for the gospel continues through his journal entries, which he left behind. One of his journal entries said this:
>
> Lord's Day, April 25th - This morning spent about two hours in sacred duties, and was enabled, more than ordinarily, to agonize for immortal souls, though it was early in the morning, and the sun scarcely shone at all, yet my body was quite wet with sweat.

Puts me to shame! Personally, I cannot remember the last time I spent 2 hours only praying for lost souls and getting drenched in sweat! Having said that I don't get drenched on the treadmill either! Was a blessing in disguise living in hot climates because while others were all dolled up and sweating in 100 degree weather, I would be chilled. I can only recall once in my life spending a night of prayer seeking salvation or knowing if an individual was truly saved. I'll discuss that later. I've spent plenty of nights praying and interceding for various topics but I require more passion to pray for the lost, especially ones I don't know. However the point is the vigor and urgency that he used to pray for the lost. Let's endeavor to reach out more and to become more passionate, especially regarding our loved ones. How much time do you spend praying for the lost or speaking to others about Christ? I believe our answers will reflect that we all need to improve our serve! _____

_____

Whether you spend eternity in heaven or hell is determined by yourself while you are still alive and able to accept Jesus Christ as your Lord and Savior. One year, I traveled from Africa to my native home in Alabama. I was serving in my Church as a French Translator for a week. I went home to visit family and met my brother who had wandered far from the way of Christ. In fact, that day, he showed me a gun and told me his intentions. I was greatly disturbed and invited him to Church. He said he was not ready for church. He'd rather get right first and be prepared to do right before engaging in church. Brethren our righteousness before the Lord is as of filthy rags. Isaiah 64.6.

I pleaded and cajoled him but nothing worked so I just prayed for him. Soon after, I returned to Congo, Africa. A short while later, I received a phone call from my Mother in the early hours of the morning announcing the death of my brother. That night, I was vexed sorely in my spirit and cried out to Almighty God. Had I not done enough to get my brother reconciled to God? Though I knew there was nothing more I could do to help my brother obtain salvation, I wanted a sign from the Lord that somehow, he had made it in.

That night was spent in fervent tears and anguish as I pleaded to the Lord regarding my brother's case. I wanted to be certain beyond a shadow of a doubt that he had entered into Eternal Life with the Lord. I wasn't sure if I could live with myself with the realization that I could have done more to bring him to salvation.

Around 6 a.m. with heaviness of heart, I dragged myself to the bathroom to shower still with no relief of knowing my brother's eternal destiny. I had to go in to work so I got dressed methodically, entered into my car and on my way to work I looked up and there was a magnificent rainbow spread across that African sky! Praise the Lord, I thought, my tears were not in vain! I thanked God because his covenant of peace covered my brother. I had no idea how he had made it in but I knew he had. The heaviness of heart and burden I had felt dissipated into thin air. Instead of mourning, it became a celebration of life for me!

When I returned to Alabama next vacation, I inquired of my eldest sister Carrie Jean, about the circumstances around our brother's death and his accepting Jesus as Lord and Savior. She unfolded a beautiful story of her husband and Father n law who were both Pastors, going into ICU while Willie lay in a coma and coaxed him back to life. The Senior Pastor asked if Willie wanted to accept Jesus as Lord and Savior to squeeze his hand. My brother did so and soon after emerged miraculously from a coma! His prognosis was good, he was in high spirits urging his estranged wayward ex-wife to take proper care of their children when she came to visit. He carried out important life decisions he had never made prior.

A few days later he was transferred to the rehabilitation center, the ambulance broke down on the way, but my family was there outside in the hot sun while he sat in the broken down ambulance laughing and joking until they were able to get him to the center. He was reportedly in good spirits. Upon arrival, he was quick to dismiss the family as they had a long drive back to their homes. He didn't turn to face them as he usually would when waving them off. The family noticed but thought he was just tired from too much heat exposure. Those were his final hours.

This incident was simply the grace of God. Similar to the thief who hung beside Jesus on the cross who made it in at the last hour (Luke 23:32-43). I'm not an expert at the game of Russian roulette, or you? Hence, I would advise while you are alive clothed in your right mind and able to make the choice to accept Jesus Christ into your life, to do so expediently.

What a triumph victory in knowing God's covenant of peace extends over the wayward family member. That God loves the bad and the good and would like all to come to salvation and the knowledge of Jesus Christ. That is why he gave his son Jesus Christ in ransom for the lost.

His Hebrew name is **Jehovah Tsidqenu – God our righteousness**, Jeremiah 23.6. We are in right standing with God only because Jesus died in our stead, resulting in Eternal life and salvation to all who believe.

Write the names of your family members, distant relatives or friends who need to be remembered as beneficiaries of the covenant of peace.

1. _____
2. _____
3. _____
4. _____
5. _____

6. _____
7. _____
8. _____
9. _____
10. _____

Now take out as much time as you need to call out each name and ask Jehovah Tsidqenu, Our Righteousness, to save him/her in the Mighty Name of Jesus.

As good as it would be to improve our serve by acts of kindness towards the lost, this will never save us! These are just *"works prepared for us in advance."*

The Covenant of Grace is found in our New Testament.

Salvation is KEY to obtaining God's promises. Without it, I could not have gone into the throne room of God to even petition on behalf of my grand-son. The Bible says, what profits a man to gain the WHOLE world but lose his soul. In other words, the state and condition of your soul is very important to God. So important that he sent his son Jesus Christ to redeem all humanity unto him.

Therefore, before we go any further in our search of obtaining divine healing. Let's look at healing for our souls.

Here are some steps to salvation taken from https://www.teenmissions.org/resources/abcs-salvation/. If you have not yet surrendered your life to Jesus Christ, asking Him to be your Lord and personal Savior, do so now with the following steps. We typically call these the **A, B, C's of Salvation.**

Admit you have Sinned

"For all have sinned and fall short of the glory of God." – Romans 3:23NKJV

"For whoever shall keep the whole law, and yet stumble in one point, he is guilty of all." – James 2:10 NKJV

"As it is written: There is none righteous, no, not one;" – Romans 3:10 NKJV

"For the wages of sin is death, but the gift of God is eternal life in Christ Jesus our Lord." – Romans 6:23 NKJV

"If we confess our sins, He is faithful and just to forgive us our sins and to cleanse us from all unrighteousness." – 1 John 1:9 NKJV

It is tough to admit that we are wrong. Even before God, we feel we are basically good, and we would like to think we are never as bad as some others. The truth is we are all sinners and can never be good enough to earn our way to heaven. God's Word, the Bible, clearly states that ALL have sinned (done things that are wrong and against God). God is holy and just. Sins against a Holy God deserve punishment. We are told in the Bible that the wages or payment for sin is death—eternal death in hell.

However, a loving, merciful God has provided a rescue plan!

Both John the Baptist and Jesus himself began their preaching with the word, '***Repent***'.

(*"Repent, for the kingdom of heaven is at hand."* –Matthew 4:17 NKJV)

To repent means 'change one's mind' or to turn — to go in another direction. How can we be led to repentance? The first step toward repentance is true sorrow for what we've done wrong. *"For Godly sorrow produces repentance leading to salvation, not to be regretted; but the sorrow of the world produces death."* – 2 Corinthians 7:10 NKJV. Worldly sorrow is more like the regret of a criminal who's just been caught whereas godly sorrow is the deep remorse or conviction that produces a change in direction. Have you ever felt convicted after doing something wrong? The Bible says that the Holy Spirit is the one that convicts us of our sin. (John 16:7-8)

Believe On Jesus Christ

"For God so loved the world that He gave His only begotten Son, that whoever believes in Him should not perish but have everlasting life. For God did not send His Son into the world to condemn the world, but that the world through Him might be saved." - John 3:16-17 NKJV

"…The time is fulfilled, and the kingdom of God is at hand. Repent, and believe in the gospel."

–Mark 1:15 NKJV

"Then Paul said, John indeed baptized with a baptism of repentance, saying to the people that they should believe on Him who would come after him, that is, on Christ Jesus."

– Acts 19:4 NKJV

21

So they said, "*Believe on the Lord Jesus Christ, and you will be saved, you and your household.*" – Acts 16:31 NKJV

And this is His commandment: "*that we should believe on the Name of His Son Jesus Christ and love one another, as He gave us (this) commandment.* – 1 John 3:23 NKJV

For by grace you have been saved through faith, and that not of yourselves; it is the gift of God, not of works, lest anyone should boast. – Ephesians 2:8-9 NKJV

Salvation is not complicated. Jesus said, "*Assuredly, I say to you, whoever does not receive the kingdom of God as a little child will by no means enter it.*" – Mark 10:15 NKJV A child simply puts their trust (faith) in the father's strong arms. Likewise, we entrust our life to Jesus Christ— believing on Him and His finished work on the cross. The Apostle Paul defined the message of the Gospel (good news) like this— "*For I delivered to you first of all that which I also received: that Christ died for our sins according to the Scriptures, and that He was buried, and that He rose again the third day according to the Scriptures,*" – 1 Corinthians 15:3-4 NKJV Jesus Christ, the perfect, sinless lamb of God, laid down His life and took the penalty meant for us, dying in our place (Isaiah 53:6). He paid the debt we could not pay and redeemed us (bought us back) from the power of sin and death. (John 1:29 / Galatians 3:13 / Romans 3:25)

List the A, B, C's of Salvation

1. _____
2. _____
3. _____

What is the meaning of to '*repent*'? _____

What is the first step towards repentance? _____

_____

Explain the difference between worldly sorrow and Godly sorrow? _____

_____

_____

Why does man need a Savior? _____

_____

What kind of Baptism did John perform? _____.
What was his announcement? _____.

What kind of Baptism does Jesus speak of? _____.

Why does Jesus say to receive the Kingdom of God like a little child? _____

_____.

What did Jesus redeem us from? _____

_____

So what happens the next time I commit a sin? Am I condemned eternally? What does Romans 8:1 say? What does that mean to you? _____

_____

_____

Nuggets Gleaned from Today's Study:

+

+

+

Session 1: Covenant

Week One/ Day Five

Confess Christ Publicly

"…that if you confess with your mouth the Lord Jesus and believe in your heart that God has raised Him from the dead, you will be saved. For with the heart one believes unto righteousness, and with the mouth confession is made unto salvation." – Romans 10:9-10 NKJV

For I am not ashamed of the gospel of Christ, for it is the power of God to salvation for everyone who believes, for the Jew first and also for the Greek. – Romans 1:16 NKJV

God did his part, sending His one and only Son to die in our place. He has offered us a free gift — salvation, the forgiveness of sin, eternal life with Him in heaven. BUT… we must receive that gift. We must confess our sins (1 John 1:9) and confess (or proclaim) our faith (belief) in the death, burial and resurrection of God's son, Jesus Christ. Confessing with our mouth requires an outward, public action, not a secret, hidden, timid faith. The Apostle Paul boldly proclaimed his faith so that others could hear and be saved. God's plan of salvation is freely offered to everyone.

These are the **ABC's of Salvation** (Ref. https://www.teenmissions.org/resources/abcs-salvation/).

I encourage you to repeat this prayer of salvation if you have never done it before. If you are a part of an Oasis group, tell one of your Leading Ladies about your decision. Find a local Church or Pastor to confide in. If you have no one to tell, write me so that I can pray for you. You can find my information at the back of this work-book.

Prayer of Salvation

Heavenly Father, I come to you in faith, I admit that I am a sinner, I cannot help myself. I believe that you are the Son of God and died for my sins, I confess right now that I have sinned and come short of your glory. Forgive me Lord. Your Word says whosoever shall call upon the name of the Lord shall be saved. Lord Jesus, I call upon your name, save me. Let your blood cleanse me. Deliver me from this life of sin & death. Write my name in the Book of Life. In Jesus Mighty Name, Amen!

I would also encourage you to forsake your life of sin, and abide in Christ! John 15:4.

In John 5:4 there was a lame man who had laid at the Pool of Bethesda for 38 years. When Jesus healed him and later saw him at the temple, he told him, in verse *14 'Afterward Jesus found him in the temple and said to him, "See, you are well! Sin no more, that nothing worse may happen to you."*

Exercise

The first is called the Old Covenant or _____, from which we name the first part of the Bible, the Latin rendering of the word covenant. The second is called the _____, or New Testament.

Brainstorm

1). What is a covenant in the legal sense?   In the Biblical sense?

_____

_____

_____

_____

2). Please read these examples of covenants in the Bible and write what you learn.

    A. Read Genesis 9:9-12. In verse 8, who was God talking to? _____.
Name the people or animals whom God mentioned that he was making a covenant with.

1). Noah

2)._____

3)._____

4)._____

5)._____

6)._____

3) In Verse 12, the Lord says this covenant was actually for generations to come. What was the sign of the covenant? _____ What would we know when we saw that sign in the sky?

List the members of your family included in that covenant. Don't forget to include your pets!

1).

2).

3).

4).

5).

6).

Although in my wildest dreams I would have NEVER imagined the ordeal that I went through during Olivier's illness. However; knowing that we were under an everlasting covenant written by a faithful and true God, I had no doubt we were well protected!

Session 2: The Promise

Week Two/ Day One

The Promise of Peace

Suggested Reading: Chapters 5-7 of Book 'Release the Dove'

Isaiah 54:9-17

"To me this is like the days of Noah,
*   when I swore that the waters of Noah would never again cover the earth.*
So now I have sworn not to be angry with you,
*   never to rebuke you again.*
[10] Though the mountains be shaken
*   and the hills be removed,*
yet my unfailing love for you will not be shaken
*   nor my covenant of peace be removed,"*
*   says the LORD, who has compassion on you.*

[13] All your children will be taught by the LORD,
*   and great will be their peace.*
[14] In righteousness you will be established:
Tyranny will be far from you;
*   you will have nothing to fear.*
Terror will be far removed;
*   it will not come near you.*

[17]   no weapon forged against you will prevail,
*   and you will refute every tongue that accuses you.*
This is the heritage of the servants of the LORD,
*   and this is their vindication from me,"*
declares the LORD.

Contrast with Genesis 9:8-17

[8] Then God said to Noah and to his sons with him: [9] "I now establish my covenant with you and with your descendants after you [10] and with every living creature that was with you—the birds, the livestock and all the wild animals, all those that came out of the ark with you—every living

creature on earth. ¹¹ *I establish my covenant with you: Never again will all life be destroyed by the waters of a flood; never again will there be a flood to destroy the earth."*

¹² *And God said, "This is the sign of the covenant I am making between me and you and every living creature with you, a covenant for all generations to come:* ¹³ *I have set my rainbow in the clouds, and it will be the sign of the covenant between me and the earth.* ¹⁴ *Whenever I bring clouds over the earth and the rainbow appears in the clouds,* ¹⁵ *I will remember my covenant between me and you and all living creatures of every kind. Never again will the waters become a flood to destroy all life.* ¹⁶ *Whenever the rainbow appears in the clouds, I will see it and remember the everlasting covenant between God and all living creatures of every kind on the earth."*

¹⁷ *So God said to Noah, "This is the sign of the covenant I have established between me and all life on the earth."*

Questions

1). In Isaiah 54:10. Based upon what you have learned about a covenant in the Biblical sense, in your own words, write out what you believe to be a "Covenant of Peace".

_____

_____

_____Who do

you believe this covenant of peace is referring

to?_____.

Turn in your Bible to Isaiah 26:3. Write that verse

here_____

_____.

God has given each of us a covenant of peace. No matter what is going on in your world, you can benefit from this covenant if only your mind is stead-fast on_____.

The entire time that Olivier was ill, I basked in the covenant of peace. Very seldom was I worried or concerned that he would not be healed. This condition existed ONLY BECAUSE I chose to keep my mind stead-fast on Christ. Remember Peter's moments of fame walking on the water? (Matthew 14:22-33) When did he begin to sink? _____

Beloved, anytime you take your eyes off of the ONE who is able to save you, deliver you, heal you, you are bound to sink! Because taking your eyes off of Jesus means your eyes are now on that sickness, financial difficulty, wayward child, loveless marriage. But when your "eyes are upon" the Word of God. When you choose to read His Word and accept His promises, it is the same as keeping your eyes on Him. Because Jesus is synonymous to His Word.

The Bible says, *"In the beginning was the Word, and the Word was with God, and the Word was God."* John 1:1

Let's memorize this verse. "In the beginning was _____ and
_____the_____. John 1:1.

Now read that verse out-loud. Let it roll off of your tongue. Enunciate each word and say it with conviction repeating where this verse is found at the end!

Well done!

Now, let's re-write this verse putting the name of Jesus in parenthesis next to "Word". Read out-loud. _____

_____

Does it make you think of that scripture differently when you see the name of Jesus there? The Bible says that every promise in Jesus is YES AND AMEN!

"For no matter how many promises God has made, they are "Yes" in Christ. And so through him the "Amen" is spoken by us to the glory of God". 2 Corinthians 1:20.

When you discover what God is for your situation or that the answer is YES know what the word Amen Amen is a transliteration of usually uttered at the end means, 'so be it.' the Word and the WILL of problem, you will realize AND AMEN. Do you means? the Hebrew word amen of a song or a prayer and it Therefore when you utter a

> *And I will do whatever you ask in my name, so that the Father may be glorified in the Son.*
>
> **John 14:13**

prayer saying amen at the end, you are in actuality decreeing it as done. Furthermore, The Lord said whatever we ask in Jesus Name, He would do it! Therefore, every prayer should end "In Jesus Name (IJN), Amen".

When I prayed for Olivier, My prayer ended mostly in Jesus name, AMEN. Most were decrees rather than supplication.

Return to Isaiah 54:13 printed out above for you. Write out the verse here_____
_____. The NASB version actually says, *"All of your sons shall be taught by the Lord and great shall be thy peace!"*

Being such a young grand-mother, my husband and I have often added Olivier to our direct lineage as being our son therefore it is easy for me to pray using verse 13. Olivier lived with us in Nigeria when he was 12 months old, Bordeaux France and Malaysia twice. We have made him a part of our immediate family.

I will show you this principle in Genesis 48.5. Write what it says inserting Olivier's name.

_____

Session 2: The Promise

Week Two/ Day Two

The Promise of Protection

The last scripture in the covenant of peace to look at is verse 17. It's a shouting verse!

Verse 17 says *no weapon forged against you will prevail,*

and you will refute every tongue that accuses you.

This is the heritage of the servants of the LORD,

and this is their vindication from me,"

declares the LORD.

This verse is a shouting verse! Because it says that no weapon of sickness, disease, financial difficulty, family issue will prevail. That word prevail means **prove more powerful or superior.**

"It is hard for logic to **prevail over** emotion."

synonyms: win, win out, win through, triumph, be victorious, be the victor, gain the victory, carry the day, carry all before one, finish first, come out ahead, come out on top, succeed, prove superior, conquer, overcome, gain/achieve mastery, gain ascendancy; (Ref. google)

In other words, no problem that you have will be victorious, succeed, conquer or overcome you! GOD HIMSELF will refute or prove false or erroneous, every charge or opinion against you!

Let us look at this meaning closer. In chapters 1-3 of *Release the Dove*, I elaborated on Olivier's illness. I also mentioned what the doctors said concerning his case.

But what did God just say in the verses we have read? He has given me a covenant of peace. My son (grand-son) would be taught by him, *mycoplasma pneumonia* would not be victorious or succeed to destroy my grandson. The Lord Himself would prove Olivier's report wrong or erroneous!

Dearly Beloved, may I caution you that you can never see God's Word in the natural but you must seek the spiritual through faith. What you see with your physical eyes are limited but what she see with your spiritual eyes are limitless!

The Bible states in Hebrews 11:6, " [6] *But without faith it is impossible to please Him, for he who comes to God must believe that He is, and that He is a rewarder of those who diligently seek Him."*

Faith is an important ingredient in the life of a believer. If you want to learn how to pray effectively, you must be available.

God told Abraham to look at the stars of the sky. "He took him outside and said, *"Look up at the sky and count the stars--if indeed you can count them." Then he said to him, "So shall your offspring be."*
His descendants would be like the stars in the sky. But wait a minute, how many stars could Abraham actually see or count? Look at the stars of the sky. How far could Abraham actually see? The Lord was counting on his spiritual insight but also the sky appeared much brighter during that era without all the extra lighting in today's known world.

Tomorrow will dawn more light on this topic.

Nuggets Gleaned from Today's Study:

   +

   +

   +

Session 2: The Promise

Week Two/ Day Three
The Promise of Descendants

I found the following to be an extraordinary observation written by Allan A. Macrae, Ph.D. I invite you to read excerpts of this piece of work done by a literary genius. Although the reading might be a little extensive, the conclusion he arrives at is quite clever and will definitely prove worth the read! Quite fascinating and I believe will bless you immensely!

ABRAHAM AND THE STARS

By: ALLAN A. MACRAE, Ph.D.

Since God, who inspired the writers of the Bible, is also the Creator of nature, it is to be expected that the Bible and nature will fit together. This, of course, does not mean that we can construct a complete science of physics, chemistry, botany, astronomy, or even history, from the study of the Bible. This not its purpose. The Bible was written to tell us what we need to know about God, about man's sin, about the possibility of reconciliation to God, and about God's plan for man. These are great and vital subjects, and it is difficult to get a true understanding of them into the heart of sinful man. To do so is the purpose of the Bible. Nevertheless, if the Bible is to fulfill this purpose, it could hardly be expected that its Divine Author would allow it to be in error with regard to other subjects. Even though the full explanation of such matters is no part of its purpose, its incidental references to them could hardly be erroneous. It is the claim of Jesus Christ and His apostles that God's Word is entirely true. This does not mean, of course, that the Bible will use the scientific terminology that is in vogue today. Such terminology changes from time to time.

What the word "science" generally meant a century ago, the word "philosophy" means today. What the word "philosophy" generally meant a century ago, the word "science" means today.

We must take words and phrases in the meanings that they possessed at the time when they were written. A similar situation exists in connection with the use of the word "day."

We do not believe that the sun goes down and up but that the earth turns; yet no one has any difficulty in understanding what we mean when we speak of sunset and sunrise. Through the ages it has been the belief of the Christian church that the statements of the Bible, if correctly and carefully interpreted, will not contradict any aspect of God's creation or of God's universe. Sometimes the incompleteness of our knowledge of some phase of science or history may cause us to think that a statement in the Bible is wrong. A little later, when our knowledge has moved forward, we are enabled to see clearly that the Biblical statement revealed a knowledge on the part of the Divine Author beyond what was known to man. The Bible is never out of date, but it is often ahead of date. This is well illustrated in the divine promise to Abraham regarding the stars. Today most people know very little about the stars. A century ago the appearance of a comet in the sky would be immediately noticed and would produce wide-spread discussion. If a comet should now appear, most people would know nothing about it, except what they read in the newspapers, or hear on the radio. The reason for this, of course, is the tremendous increase in the lighting of our streets. During the last fifty years artificial light has become so strong and so extensive in most of our populated areas that very few people ever get more than a tiny glimpse of the stars. It is an entirely different situation from that of a century ago, when everybody saw a great deal of the stars and most people came to know the major constellations almost as if they were friends. We can be sure that Abraham had this sort of knowledge. There was hardly any artificial lighting in the areas where he spent most of his time. He was often outdoors when the heavens were covered with brilliant stars and must have known a good deal about them. In addition Abraham had come from Ur of the Chaldees and had spent a large part of his life in Haran. Both of these were towns that were dedicated to worship of the moon god. Babylonian astronomy and astrology were widely cultivated. Even though one held an entirely different religion, he could hardly spend years in a Babylonian environment without knowing a good deal about the stars, to say nothing of the many observations that he would naturally make during long evenings in the out-of-doors, undisturbed by the artificial light that now keeps most of us from paying much attention to them. In view of all this, it must have been a very great surprise to Abraham when God gave him the particular promise recorded in Genesis 15:5. In Genesis 12:3. God had already promised Abraham that He would make him a great nation. Having lived in the great nations of Mesopotamia, Abraham would hardly think of a group of a few thousand people as being a great nation. He must certainly have thought that this promise meant much more than that. Yet in Genesis 15, when Abraham was enduring depression and discouragement, the Lord directed him to look at the stars, saying: "Look now toward heaven, and tell (count) the stars, if thou be able to number them." And he said unto him, "So shall thy seed be" (Genesis 15:5). This must have impressed Abraham as a very strange promise. He could hardly have been ignorant of the fact that all the stars that can be seen with the naked eye from any place in the Near East would total well under 4,000 (and no one in that day would have any reason to think that stars existed that could not be seen with the naked eye). Four thousand might appear like a large number of dots, but it would hardly represent "a great nation." Abraham may have thought: "Look at the wonderful beauty of the stars. God has promised that I am going to have descendants who will shine like the stars, and will be indeed a heavenly progeny." Yet as he thought it over, he would know that this was a mere rationalization. After all, God had said: "Look toward heaven and count the stars, if thou be able to number them; ... so shall thy seed be." It was not a difficult task to number the stars that could be seen with the naked eye. More than three thousand years were yet to pass before the telescope would be invented and it would be possible to learn that there are far more stars than the naked eye can see. In Genesis 17:5 God promised Abraham that he would become "a father of many nations." This must indeed have seemed incongruous to Abraham, after the comparison of his descendants to the number of the stars. Four thousand descendants would not be enough for one great nation, and certainly not enough for many nations. In chapter 22 God repeated His promise to Abraham, saying, in verse 17: "I will multiply thy seed as the stars of the heaven, and as the sand which is upon the sea shore." Now," Abraham may have said, "here is a real promise! Who can count the sand that is on the seashore? If my descendants are to be as numerous as the seashore, I shall indeed have a tremendous progeny!" More than three thousand years passed, and then the telescope was invented. Soon men were able to observe great numbers of previously unknown stars. According to the latest estimates, there are about two hundred billion stars in our galaxy alone. Within the present century it has been found that our galaxy is only one of millions of galaxies, each of which also contains great numbers of stars.

At this point a question may reasonably be asked. Are we assuming certain things about Abraham's knowledge for which we have no proof? Can we be sure that Abraham knew so much about Babylonian astronomy? Can we be sure that Babylonians had counted the stars as early as the time of Abraham? Is it not possible that Abraham actually knew very little about the stars and that from merely glancing at them he received the impression of a tremendous number and therefore considered it a marvelous promise that his descendants would be as numerous as the stars Only after the telescope was invented were we able to see that the Bible was right all along.

God who is the Creator of nature is also the Author of the Bible. He knows many facts that science never dreamed of in Abraham's day. He knows many facts that science has not yet discovered. If, as was formerly true in this case, a clear statement in the Bible disagrees with a present observation or theory of science, let's just wait until science discovers more facts. Genesis 15:5 is very appropriately followed by the words: "And he believed in the Lord; and He counted it to him for righteousness." **Faith Theological Seminary Elkins Park, Pa.** / Allan A. Macrae, PHD

God who is the Creator of nature is also the Author of the Bible.

Allow some time for reflection. Please share here in a short paragraph how the reading above has affected your knowledge of who God is.

_____

_____

_____

_____

_____

Now in regards to my covenant of peace. It could also be said that "And Rhonda _____

_____ *Gen 15.5*

Beloved, because something does not appear real to you, because the sign of the rainbow on the occasion of our wedding, then my brother's funeral and other times I have not even mentioned--- does not seem logical to you, doesn't mean it isn't real. I can mention several other occasions where the rainbow showed up -a decision on which school my son should attend, a change of jobs for my husband, a decision of a change of job or location for my daughter, the end of a one week conference where I was the keynote speaker.........the occurrences are often when we are at a cross-roads and don't know which way to go, God reminds us of his covenant of peace. My children all know about this covenant of peace. They also take notice when a rainbow shows up. My grand-son is aware but not my grand-daughter though she has offered me 'rainbow drawings' before, as if she knew! Now insert your name in faith: Genesis 15:5 _____

_____

In the lengthy text on pages 31-33, underline or high-light everything that points to *Abraham's Promise.*

What did the Bible say in reference to what Abraham believed?

From the reading, why do you think his belief was so incredulous?

Abraham received so much ONLY because he chose to belief God and was upright in the sight of God. Think about that. Even when it wasn't rational to do. He gained such a great reward for believing against all hope, not looking at his circumstances rather believing God's promise to him.

If Abraham's reward was great for believing God, what will yours be?

If you have areas of doubt and disbelief in your life. Deal with those issues now. Ask the Lord to give you an extra measure of faith to believe and rid yourself of doubt. Imagine Abraham in his day, trusting God that his descendants would be as numerous as the stars yet he and his wife Sarah were old and did not have children. Physically, it was IMPOSSIBLE for Sarah to conceive. Remember what is impossible with man is possible with God (Mark 10.27). Be prepared to experience the miraculous. Just believe!

Use this Space here to record your thoughts and prayer.

Nuggets Gleaned from Today's Study:

+

+

+

Session 2: The Promise

Week Two/ Day Four

Behold the Promise comes BUT It takes Faith!

Speaking of Abraham it says in Genesis 15:5 "And he believed in the Lord; and He counted it to him for righteousness."

This is what it says in Romans 4:16-26

Therefore, the promise comes by faith, so that it may be by grace and may be guaranteed to all Abraham's offspring—not only to those who are of the law but also to those who have the faith of Abraham. He is the father of us all. [17] *As it is written: "I have made you a father of many nations."* [c] *He is our father in the sight of God, in whom he believed—the God who gives life to the dead and calls into being things that were not.*

[18] *Against all hope, Abraham in hope believed and so became the father of many nations, just as it had been said to him, "So shall your offspring be."* [d] [19] *without weakening in his faith, he faced the fact that his body was as good as dead—since he was about a hundred years old—and that Sarah's womb was also dead.* [20] *Yet he did not waver through unbelief regarding the promise of God, but was strengthened in his faith and gave glory to God,* [21] *being fully persuaded that God had power to do what he had promised.* [22] *This is why "it was credited to him as righteousness."* [23] *The words "it was credited to him" were written not for him alone,* [24] *but also for us, to whom God will credit righteousness—for us who believe in him who raised Jesus our Lord from the dead.* [25] *He was delivered over to death for our sins and was raised to life for our justification.*

A very important component which I would like to establish here is that of FAITH. The Bible says this in Hebrews 11:6 *"And without faith it is impossible to please God, because anyone who comes to him must believe that he exists and that he rewards those who earnestly seek him."*

Write out the missing scripture: "And without faith it is _____ to please God, because anyone who comes to him must _____ that he exists and that he _____ those who earnestly seek him. Hebrews_____.

What exactly is Faith? Find out by reading from the book which is often referred to as the Hall of Faith, Hebrews 11:1. Notice the various translation of this verse.

Faith shows the reality of what we hope for; it is the evidence of things we cannot see. NLT

Now faith is the substance of things hoped for, the evidence of things not seen. NKJV

Now faith is the assurance of things hoped for, the conviction of things not seen. ESV

Now faith is the assurance (title deed, confirmation) of things hoped for (divinely guaranteed), and the evidence of things not seen [the conviction of their reality—faith comprehends as fact what cannot be experienced by the physical senses]. Amplified

Now in YOUR OWN WORDS from what you have read, write out what faith is to you. You might want to use an illustration or an example of something that has taken place in your own life.

_____

_____

_____

_____

Whole books have been written on this topic however the book which has influenced me the most is one written by Kenneth Hagin in 1966 titled simply, **What Faith Is.** This book is not large in content nor long in pages. Yet its message alone has carried me through nearly 30 years as I have endeavored to live a life of Faith. I would recommend this book to each and every one of you as a basic to keep in your personal library. It is small enough to even keep in your purse during a time of crisis! Read it! What affects me the most is testimonies about others and how they obtained divine healing from God. This book is HIS testimony and a model that I subconsciously used during my grandson's illness.

I refer to Kenneth Hagin as "*The Modern Day Father of Faith*". You can down-load much of his material free. He has many books ranging from healing, the Holy Spirit, visions and many others. They are small enough to read in a day but packed with encouragement and faith for a life-time!

How do I get faith? James 1:5-8 NLT gives us a clue.

"*⁵ If you need wisdom, ask our generous God, and he will give it to you. He will not rebuke you for asking. ⁶ But when you ask him, be sure that your faith is in God alone. Do not waver, for a person with divided loyalty is as unsettled as a wave of the sea that is blown and tossed by the wind. ⁷ Such people should not expect to receive anything from the Lord.⁸ their loyalty is divided between God and the world, and they are unstable in everything they do.*"

So HOW do you get the faith you need for God to do the things in your life or the lives of your love ones? _____ Now give that prayer "*feet*" by praying your request using a verse that validates it.

_____

_____

_____

Well done! Excellent work for today. We will speak more on praying scripture verses and knowing God's willing to heal you in the following chapters!

Session 2: The Promise

Week Two/Day Five

The Promise to get Faith!

There is a wonderful verse in Romans 10:17 that says this:

Consequently, faith comes from hearing the message, and the message is heard through the word about Christ.

In Biology class we were taught that Osmosis is a process by which molecules of a solvent tend to pass through a semipermeable membrane from a less concentrated solution into a more concentrated one.

In layman terms and in relation to the topic at hand, Osmosis is the process of gradual or unconscious assimilation of ideas, knowledge, etc.

We have just read that faith comes from hearing the message, and the message (of faith) is heard through the Word of Christ.

Beloved, it is only natural if you spend hours listening to the Presidential debates on television, this is where your faith will lie. What you watch and listen to will have an indelible effect on what you believe. Therefore I would admonish you to spend this day soaking in faith.

I suggest free readings or downloads from Kenneth Hagin who I fondly refer to as the "*Modern Day Father of Faith*".

Here is the website: http://www.rhema.org/

He also has a site on Nutrition, DO NOT GET side-tracked! Stay focused! Enjoy your Faith read. Share with your group what you have gleaned from your independent study!

Notes

Topic: _____

Session 3: The Preparation for the Task Ahead

Suggested Reading: Chapter 8 of Book 'Release the Dove'

Week Three/ Day One

Talitha Koum Arise Conference

If each of us would know what our future holds, would you live differently? I can count off several times in my life when the Holy Spirit prepared me for an unknown task ahead. Much depended on my obedience. This time was no different.

Firstly, the preceding year to Olivier's illness which was 2014, I was asked by my Church to organize a Women's Conference. This entailed not only coming up with a theme but also organizing speakers and the entire event! Being a natural at organization was not the issue. But I needed to hear from God on what the topic would be! As I sat directly behind my Pastor (Amos) in one of our sister Churches during their Thanksgiving Service, the Lord dropped Talitha Koum in my Spirit. I knew this verse and quickly thumbed through my Bible to find it!

Mark 5:41 says, *"He took her by the hand and said to her, "Talitha Koum!" (which means "Little girl, I say to you, get up!"*

So this became our Theme for our Women's Conference in 2014. I meditated on the scripture and built an entire conference around it. The Word was buried deep in my spirit. Fast forward almost 1 year to the date, Olivier is evacuated to Singapore. I left the hospital and went to my friend's home to grab a few hours of sleep. I awoke and instantly looked at the clock's dial which was right in my face! It read 5.34. Initially, I didn't think that time would be significant but the clock's face showed the digital time, the illuminous numbers seared into my subconscious.

I was only concerned about getting dressed and getting downstairs in time to catch a ride with my friend's husband, William, to the hospital. He became such an encouragement to me on those rides and his wife Shereen was so efficient, providing all that I needed without my asking. They were such a huge blessing to my family and I for the duration of this ordeal and even afterwards.

As I sat and waited for William, the Holy Spirit brought to my remembrance once more the clock's dial, then beckoned me to look for that scripture in Mark 5.34. I quickly took my Bible out of my bag and found the scripture. Please write what it says: _____

_____

It was as if the Lord was giving me clues and had set me up, for what I wasn't entirely sure. But I understood one thing, it would be my faith that would get Olivier's healing and he would be whole! Praise the Lord! In the story of the woman with the issue of blood, she risked her faith to go out into a crowd where she could have been stoned to death. She had been bleeding for many years, had used all of the available funds she had to see doctors but rather grew worse! But one day, she heard Jesus was coming into town and risked her faith to meet him! She said within herself, if only I could touch the hem of his garment I would be made whole.

Let us see what we can learn from this woman's encounter which can bring about wholeness. Some have received fragmented healings which have left their physical bodies whole but their minds unhealed. This woman had suffered much! Imagine living a lonely life apart from family and friends! Imagine being ostracized and possibly being reduced to begging! She must have been a woman of sustenance to have visited so many doctors, but yet NOW her sickness reduced her possibly to a life as a street urchin.

The Bible says in 3 John 2 in the New Living Translation:

² Beloved, I pray that in every way you may succeed and prosper and be in good health [physically], just as [I know] your soul prospers [spiritually].

According to this verse, how would God have us to prosper? _____ & _____

In the Message Bible Psalms 103 reads:

¹⁻² O my soul, bless GOD.
  From head to toe, I'll bless his holy name!
O my soul, bless GOD,
  don't forget a single blessing!

³⁻⁵ He forgives your sins—every one.
  He heals your diseases—every one.
  He redeems you from hell—saves your life!
  He crowns you with love and mercy—a paradise crown.
  He wraps you in goodness—beauty eternal.
  He renews your youth—you're always young in his presence.

⁶⁻¹⁸ GOD makes everything come out right;
  he puts victims back on their feet.

In this passage in verse one, who or what did the psalmist address: _____

List the benefits and blessings from this passage.

1.

2.

3.

4.

5.

6.

7.

Now many of you who know me well also know that I'm shouting at this point! Praise God for the benefits in blessing His Holy Name!

Beloved, God wants us to be whole - Mind, Body & Spirit. As a human being, you were first given a body, then a spirit (reference Genesis 2:7). Without getting too deep into the tripartite perspective, I would like to bring to your attention, Hebrews 4: 12.

[2] For the word of God is living and active, sharper than any two-edged sword, piercing to the division of soul and of spirit, of joints and of marrow, and discerning the thoughts and intentions of the heart.

Write the 3 components of the Human Body

1.

2.

3.

According to scriptures we have read, what do you think involves making a person whole?

_____ *If you were to look within yourself, what would be necessary to make you feel whole?* _____

_____

_____

Fill in the blank from Hebrews 4:12 "For the _____ (   ) of God is living and active.....What is living and active? _____*Recall our previous exercise, what did we write in parenthesis?*

*Write your first memory verse here. I'll give you a hint. John 1:1:*_____

_____.

My precious friends in Christ, only our Savior, Jesus Christ, is able to make you completely whole. He healed the woman with the issue of blood and made her whole. He healed Olivier and made him whole. List the names of the people you desire to receive wholeness and repeat this following prayer on their behalf.

Names of people needing to be made whole

1.

2.

3.

4.

5.

Lord Jesus, thank you today for your Word. It says that you desire to make us completely whole. Please make (cite the names above) whole today as you did with the woman with the issue of blood and as you did with Olivier! In Jesus Mighty Name, Amen!

Only God alone can discern and heal your body, spirit and soul. This is what He did for the Woman with the issue of Blood in Mark 5:34 and this is what he did with Olivier!

Olivier had always been a very shy boy similar to both his Mom and Dad, he received a double dose of shyness! Yet emerging from this illness, to his parents and our enormous surprise, Olivier is doing things we thought he would NEVER have done in the past! He auditioned to sing a solo, he recently ran for Class Rep and had to give a speech! All of this from a shy boy who used to run and hide when people came into the house!

The nanny and I first noticed this new lease on life when Olivier returned from the hospital. Living next to the Twin Towers and Park in KL, we always used to try to get Olivier to exercise and play in the park to our chagrin! A friend visiting from the U.S. remarked as they walked from KLCC to our apartment, less than 10 minutes away, Olivier had even wanted to take a taxi! Taxis normally didn't like going that short distance due to the proximity! Yet after Olivier was made whole, he loved and SUGGESTED walking to the park! He desired to do life giving activities to his heart's content! He no longer relished playing video games and even put his phone aside! Medicine might make you well but only Jesus can make you whole!

What do you think Genesis 15.5 means when it says referring to Abraham, 'counted it to him for righteousness?' _____

_____

Think back to the Hebrew name of God which gives us as Christians, a righteous position before God. Write it here. _____.

It stands to reason that God sees us as He saw Abraham. Let's reach for the stars!

Please finish today learning our 2nd Memory verse. Write Hebrews 4:12 here:

Take time to memorize this passage of scripture. You might want to write it a few times from memory.

Session 3: The Preparation for the Task Ahead

Week Three/ Day Two

Olivier's Decision to get Baptized

The Preparation for the Task Ahead also involved a simple act on Olivier's behalf which I only noted of significance after the fact. Shortly after Olivier arrived in KL for the second time, we had Baptisms in our church. When the announcement was made, Olivier told me he wanted to be baptized. I was very surprised and not sure whether at 9 years of age he truly understood the signification of such an act of Faith! He said he did! I invited him to speak with the Pastor which he also did promptly. As the Baptism would take place in the afternoon, there was no time to contact Olivier's parents to inform them about his decision. We were around 12/13 hours ahead of them. Somehow in our spirit, his Grand-Father and I felt that the child was ready. So the glorious baptism took place! You would recall that in Chapter 4 in *"Release the Dove"* after serving communion to Olivier was the only thing that caused his fever to go down! Had he not been baptized, I wouldn't have been able to serve him communion.

Below is excerpted from "Taking the Plunge" from Keep Believing Ministries.

If the meaning of baptism could be boiled down to one word, that word would be identification. Baptism speaks primarily of a personal, public identification with Jesus Christ.

In Romans 6:3-4 the Apostle Paul puts the matter this way:

Don't you know that all of us who were baptized into Christ were baptized into his death? We were therefore buried with him through baptism into death in order that, just as Christ was raised from the dead through the glory of the Father, we too may live a new life.

Notice the strength of the expressions—"baptized into Christ" and "baptized into his death" and "buried with him in baptism." Someone may suggest that the primary reference here is to Spirit baptism. That's true, but at the very least, water baptism is in the background of this passage.

How important is your baptism? It is your personal identification with the greatest act of human history—the death, burial and resurrection of Jesus Christ. Baptism doesn't save you—salvation comes by faith alone (Ephesians 2:8-9). Your guilt before God is removed the moment you trust in Christ. But baptism is your personal testimony to, and the inward assurance of, your passage from the old life to the new life....

In *"Taking the Plunge"* the writer says you are literally 'preaching' the gospel when you get baptized! I love that! Read the excerpt below and find how one "preaches" when one 'plunges'. Now write down what baptism signifies using the A, B, and C's. I've given you some clues.

A. As you **ASCEND** to the water: _____

B. As you go **BELOW** into the water: _____

C. As you **COME** up out of the water: _____

Can you remember the A, B, and C's of Salvation?

A.

B.

C.

Finally, the testimony of church history is that immersion was indeed the mode of baptism practiced in the early church.

What, then, does baptism mean?

1. It means we have turned from the old life of sin to a new life in Jesus Christ.

2. It means we are publicly identifying with the death, burial and resurrection of Christ.

3. It means we are openly joining the ranks of those who believe in Christ.

According to *Taking the Plunge*, when you are baptized, you are in fact visually preaching the gospel. As you stand in the water waiting to be baptized, A, you symbolize Jesus dying on the cross. As you are lowered into the water, B, you symbolize Jesus buried in the tomb. As you are raised from the water, C, you symbolize Jesus rising from the dead.

And since you personally are being baptized, you are also saying, "I died with Jesus Christ, I was buried with him and now I am raised with Christ to brand-new life."

In short, in your baptism you are preaching a sermon without using any words at all. And your sermon in your baptism will be more effective with your friends than any sermon the pastor preaches on Sunday morning—more effective because it comes directly from you.

The Greek word translated "baptize" is the verb baptizo. According to most contemporary lexicons, the primary meaning is "to dip, plunge, immerse." The secondary meaning is to "bring under the influence."

A brief survey of baptism in the New Testament reveals the following interesting facts:

Please draw a line to the corresponding scripture.

Baptism requires water	Romans 6:4
Baptism required plenty of water.	Matthew 3:11
Baptism requires coming up out of the water	John 3:30
Baptism is called a "burial"	Matthew 3:16

Well done! I daresay, you have a message ready to preach the gospel to your neighbor, friend or family member! It's just as easy as **A, B, C & 1, 2, 3**!

I'll discuss three other important tasks that prepared me unknowingly to pray during Olivier's sickness.

Nuggets Gleaned from Today's Study:

+

+

+

Session 3: The Preparation for the Task Ahead

Week Three/ Day Three

Communion

Please read in your Bibles 1 Corinthians 11: 24-27. If Water Baptism identifies us with Christ, what does Holy Communion signify?

_____.

Do you recall what a covenant is in the Biblical sense? Look back in your notes. What does it say in John 6:51? _____

Now read Isiah 53:5 - Why was Jesus wounded_____

_____According to verse 5, how is one healed?

_____

_____.

When Olivier was ill, my constant prayer was done by pleading the blood of Jesus over him. I reminded the Lord that it was by HIS stripes that Olivier was healed. Olivier having taken the plunge was a symbolic sign of his identifying with the death, burial and resurrection of Jesus Christ. Taking communion was a way for Olivier to remember what Jesus did for him in His body so that he might be healed. Communion is important for so many reasons. One of those is to nullify sickness in your body.

1 Corinthians 11:27-30 English Standard Version (ESV)

27 Whoever, therefore, eats the bread or drinks the cup of the Lord in an unworthy manner will be guilty concerning the body and blood of the Lord. 28 Let a person examine himself, then, and so eat of the bread and drink of the cup. 29 For anyone who eats and drinks without discerning the body eats and drinks judgment on himself. 30 That is why many of you are weak and ill, and some have died.[a]

Through Communion, people can be healed of many various diseases and illnesses. The way a believer takes Communion can directly affect his or her health. Please open to 1 Corinthians 11:27-30, again, this time we'll read from the New International Version, emphasis added).

"Therefore, whoever eats the bread or drinks the cup of the Lord in an unworthy manner will be guilty of sinning against the body and blood of the Lord. A man ought to examine himself before he eats of the bread and drinks of the cup. For anyone who eats and drinks without recognizing the body of the Lord eats and drinks judgment on himself. That is why many among you are weak and sick, and a number of you have fallen asleep."

What do you think it means to recognize or discern the body of Christ?

_____

_____

What are ways that we can "eat or drink" judgment on ourselves by taking the communion in an "unworthy fashion?"

1.

2.

3.

Communion also referred to as the Lord's Supper, originated in Jesus' last observance of Passover, the night before His crucifixion. During that meal, Jesus shared a cup of wine, and said it was the new covenant in His blood, for the forgiveness of our sins. He also broke bread and said it represented His body.

You might recall the miracle of the 5 loaves and 2 fish. Barley is the first grain to be harvested in the spring, and the feast of unleavened bread celebrates the first fruits of the barley harvest. Jesus performs this miracle as Passover approaches, and will go on later in John 6 to explain that he himself is the bread of life (*Above Ref. Sid Roth, Healing through Communion, Mar 1, 2006*).

Later Jesus used that passage to teach on his body being bread that came down from heaven. Jesus took 39 stripes on his back. According to Dr. Dale Robbins' teachings, every medical illness can be categorized under 39 headings. Whether this is fact or fallacy is irrelevant because we know that the blood of Jesus suffices to cleanse you of every malady.

I am the Bread of Life -JESUS

Reflections

If you have not been baptized by full immersion or if you don't take communion, I hope this chapter will enable you to make a firm decision today once you see all the wonderful benefits.

List some of the benefits of being baptized and partaking in communion:

1.

2.

3.

5.

6.

Jesus has literally taken the beating due us for our sin. Discerning the body of the Christ means our focus should be on the Lord and we should recognize what his dying on the cross meant for us! He took sickness upon his body so that we would not be sick. The Bible says by his stripes we were healed. That is past tense. Please understand healing has already been given to us. We just need to accept it in our bodies! Jesus has already paid the price for our healing by the

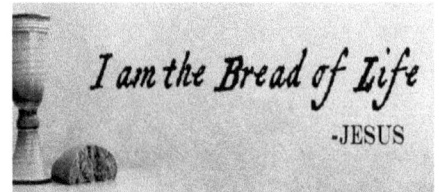

scourging He experienced, so that we do not have to be sick! Isaiah talked about a coming Messiah who would take our sins and our sicknesses onto His own body. Chapter 53 of the book of Isaiah describes what the ancient rabbis referred to as the leprous Messiah, because early portions of the chapter talk about His being marred or disfigured by all the sin and disease of humanity. *"Surely our griefs [sickness, Heb.] He Himself bore, and our sorrows [Heb., pains] He carried....But He was pierced through for our transgressions, He was crushed for our iniquities; The chastening for our well-being fell upon Him, **And by His scourging we are healed.**"* (Isaiah 53:4-5, New American Standard version, emphasis added).

This passage is repeated in Matthew 8:17 and in 1 Peter 2:24 because it is so important. Jesus took our sin and died to pay the price, and by the wounds in His body, we have been healed. When we discern His body, we are to consider this important fact. In the Communion supper, the Lord provided two elements, wine and bread. As we take the wine, which represents His blood, we are forgiven of our sin. As we eat the bread, we are healed in our bodies. God gave us this physical ceremony in Communion, for the healing of our physical bodies, as well as for the forgiveness of our sins (*Ref. Sid Roth Healing through Communion, Mar 1, 2006).*

From the reading, brainstorm this exercise.	What is it a Representation of or another word for:	Bible Reference
Wine		
Bread		
39 stripes		
Coming Messiah		
Barley		
Fish		
Communion		
Discern		
chastening		
5 loaves		

The last two very important elements that prepared me for the tasks ahead will be discussed tomorrow.

But I must warn you, the next few days might be challenging for certain people especially those who are still waiting for answered prayer or for those who have lost battles resulting in unanswered prayers. I would say to those people, what '**Word**' has the Lord given you? For me it was Mark 5.34. This scripture says, *'Woman your faith has made you whole'* referring to the woman with the issue of blood.

Jesus does the healing but it took my faith to grasp the Word of God, stand and believe despite sheer opposition. In my case, my grandson was engulfed with lifesaving paraphernalia connected to his lifeless body. It took a miracle and it took God to intervene. I literally not only had to act in the spiritual but also in the natural. I prevented the doctors from carrying out treatments meant to cure Olivier yet were doing the very opposite because I held on to the Word of God. This is the joyful outcome of my story which I am sharing with you primarily to give my God the glory but also in hopes of helping others who are hopeless.

For instance, we started a pilot study of this workbook in late January 2017. I had invited my neighbor whose daughter was suffering from an idiopathic disease which presented with the formation of tumors in various parts of her body. Doctors where we live had taken a 'wait and see approach'. After attending only one meeting, this Mom was motivated into seeking more answers for her daughter. My book fueled her and prompted her into returning to the USA raising thousands of dollars to help cure her daughter.

The woman in Mark 5.34 had an issue. Her issue had to do with hemorrhaging. Whether your issue is physical or spiritual, I would encourage you to seek a Word from God. The Word, *'Woman, your faith has made you whole,'* was more than enough for me.

Let faith arise oh God, in the lives of those holding on to this book and desiring a miracle! For those who are standing in faith, comfort them and give them a WORD today to sustain them throughout their ordeal. Whatever their outcome, allow them to see you as you are, 'A good, good Father.' In Jesus Mighty Name, Amen!

Oftentimes, when I cannot trace God and I do not know what He is doing, I return to the "***Hall of Faith***" in Chapter 11 of Hebrews. In the final words of that chapter lies our eternal hope.

Spend some time today praying over your list of names from page 40.

Session 3: The Preparation for the Task Ahead

Week Three/ Day Four

Prayer Surmount

Two Chinese sisters whom are both very dear to me and attend our Women's Bible Study extended an invitation to a prayer surmount at their Church. They had also invited me in past years but obligations in my local church always conflicted with the appointment. This time, checking the calendar, I decided I would attend! It also corresponded with my statement made to our Bible Study ladies regarding fasting and prayer. For Easter I sometimes prepare by fasting. This year, our ladies had a challenge of praying for our husbands for 40 days. I decided that I wanted to be on a "Word Fast". I was seeking deep revelation from God. I so wanted to be saturated in His Word. I made this public declaration to the group.

I was so excited about going to the Chinese Church however I received a message from our Pastor asking everyone to attend an impromptu prayer meeting on the same day I had planned to go with my two Chinese sisters! To make matters even more complicated, I was on the prayer roster to lead prayers! I had to make a decision, whether to honor my commitment at the Chinese Church or fulfill my duty in my home Church. I pondered and prayed about the matter before responding to my Pastor excusing myself by informing him of the prior engagement I felt impelled to attend.

I felt drained spiritually and really needed a boost. Turned out going to Ruth and Mei Leng's Church provided the boost I needed! We started around 6 a.m. and prayed till 2 pm! Pastor Suba, from Kenya, came with such fire and revelation that by the time I left Church, I was filled to the brim and overflowing! All of the following week, I prayed constantly and at '*all times*'. The next Saturday, I returned to the Chinese Church though there was no particular program. I just felt lead to be incognito and lay prostrate before the Lord with no demands to lead. I went with my friend Dorothy; together we enjoyed the presence of the Lord. It was on that same day arriving home before noon that Olivier brought me the thermometer registering a high fever! When I reflect back to that time: I wonder if I had NOT been obedient to attend *The Prayer Surmount*, would I have had the strength to sustain the lengthy bout of illness Olivier had? If I had not been fasting and praying and if I had not proclaimed a Word fast, would I have been sensitive enough to the Spirit? I would like to create a parenthesis here.

Please list the 4 things that I believe prepared me for the task ahead.

1.

2.

3.

4.

Beloved, my '*preparations*' for Olivier's healing were not understood by me at the time. It is only when I reflect on these points '*ensemble*' that I see the connection. I point them out to encourage you to be spiritually alert. My Pastor in KL often said, "One week from Church makes one weak" and he is so right! When you do not have your spiritual antenna plugged to the Rhema Word of God, you can become dry and complacent quite easily. Think of charging your

Spiritual battery as purchasing fuel for your car. When the fuel runs out, your car can't move. If you don't do proper maintenance on your vehicle, it won't run as smoothly as it should. The same principal applies to your lap-top for all computer savvy people out there! If you don't keep your computer updated when it requests it or if you don't put an anti-virus program on your computer, it won't run as smooth as it should! Believe me, I know! Therefore, I encourage you to remain prayed up as much as possible.

Purpose is Power!

Conclude this day in prayer being sensitive to the Spirit. Is the Lord asking you to prepare or do a certain thing?

What is the last assignment He gave you?

Are you still doing it?

Remember not to get ahead of God. Purpose is power!

Nuggets Gleaned from Today's Study:

+

+

+

Session 3: The Preparation for the Task Ahead

Week Three/ Day Five

Prayer Strategies I gleaned from the Prayer Surmount ran by Pastor Suba

- *Xian Jai (Xian Jai means instructions in Chinese) - Instructions given to Israelites before going into the Promised Land, circumcision, repentance and Passover communion.*

   1   *Before praying you need to circumcise meaning to cut off everything that is unnecessary. 'Therefore, since we are surrounded by such a huge crowd of witnesses to the life of faith let us strip off every weight that slows us down, especially the sin that so easily trips us up. And let us run with endurance the race God has set before us.' Hebrews 12: 1 NLT*

   2   *Repentance means to turn away from sin. Before entering into prayer, a good practice is to repent from any known or unknown sins. "The end of all things is at hand; therefore be self-controlled and sober-minded for the sake of your prayers." 1 Peter 4:7.*

   3   *Passover Communion – In taking communion you are renewing and reactivating the covenant between us and God. Any covenant that stays idle loses its power. In communion, we are communing with His presence.*

- *After the Israelites performed the above they went into Jericho and brought the walls down with only a shout! Whatever "walls" of sickness, family issues, government issues can be brought down by using these principles listed above. Reference Joshua 6.*
- *The contrast is what happened during their battle with Ai in the very next chapter, Joshua 7 (Excerpt below taken from* https://bible.org/book/export/html/299).

After such a wonderful experience at Jericho, chapter 7 is surprising to say the least. Suddenly we are presented with a series of failures that stand in striking contrast to the victories of the past six chapters. But how instructive this is if we only have the ears to listen to the message of this chapter. The thrill of victory was so quickly replaced with the agony of defeat. Here is the story of life and one we must learn to deal with in our daily walk because this passage is so typical of most of us. One minute we can be living in victory—the next in defeat. Never is the believer in greater danger of a fall than after a victory.

We see that the Lord held the whole camp of Israel accountable for the act of one man and withheld His blessing until the matter was corrected. There was sin in the camp and God would not continue blessing the nation as long as this was so. This does not mean this was the only sin and the rest of the nation was sinless, but this sin was of such a nature (direct disobedience and rebellion) that God used it to teach Israel and us a couple of important lessons.

God viewed the nation of Israel as a unit. What one did was viewed as a sin for the whole nation because Israel's corporate life illustrates truth and warnings for us as individuals (1 Cor. 10). As a warning for the church, it shows us we cannot progress and move ahead for the Lord with known sin in our lives because that constitutes rebellion against the Lord's direction and control (Eph. 4:30; 1 Thess. 5:19). It is a matter of loving the world—and to do so is to make one behave as though he or she was an enemy of God (Jam. 4).

Please read and discuss the scriptures in the text above. Write any nuggets here.

- ➢
- ➢
- ➢

51

Looking within, what are some things you need to circumcise in your life?

Complete the blanks from the text above:

The thrill of _____ was so quickly replace with the agony of
_____.

Has this ever played out in your life?   Do you care to record a specific memory here you don't mind sharing for the edification of your small group?

_____

_____

_____

_____

Do you think it was fair that the Israelites lost the battle of Ai because of one measly person? Why or why not? _____

_____

_____

What does this tell you about the character of God? _____

_____

Many believers think that we can dwell in sin under the umbrella of grace and expect blessings to roll in. Beloved, please know that the question of sin was taken care of on the cross of Calvary once and for all. But for living a life pleasing to the Lord, obedience is better than sacrifice. Many of my Bible Scholars can recall Samuel the Prophet scolding Saul when he chose his own path instead of God's (1 Samuel 15.22). What does Galatians 6.7 tell us?
_____. Yet just as God presented the tree of the knowledge of Good and Evil to Adam and Eve in the Garden of Eden, he presents a choice of whether we want to obey or disobey. The wages of sin is death but the gift of God is eternal life (Romans 6:23). What does Revelations 22:15 say? _____

_____

God's desire is that we present our bodies as a living sacrifice holy and acceptable to God, this is your true and proper worship (Romans 12: 1-2).

Our 3rd memory verse comes from Hebrews 12:1a. Write it here and practice memorizing it.

_____

_____

_____

"12 So the one who thinks he is standing firm should be careful not to fall. 13 No temptation has seized you except what is common to man. And God is faithful; He will not let you be tempted beyond what you can bear. But when you are tempted, He will also provide an escape, so that you can stand up under it." 1 Corinthians 10:1-13.

Conclude with a prayer citing out loud to God (alone) the sins that so easily trip you up. Repent which means to _____. Ask the Holy Spirit to help you to steer clear.

Use this space to record your prayer:

Unity of Spirit is an underlying force in powerful prayer. The Bible says in 1 Peter 3:7 Berean Study Bible, *"Husbands, in the same way, treat your wives with consideration as a delicate vessel, and with honor as fellow heirs of the gracious gift of life, so that your prayers will not be hindered.* Your husband should be your strongest prayer partner in times of intense warfare. If you are married, try to employ this scripture as often as possible. You will be surprised will your results!

My next chapter will be on how to pray right, not amiss and standing in the Gap!

Nuggets Gleaned from Today's Study:

⁜

⁜

⁜

<u>Session 4: How to Pray right, not Amiss, Pray Effectively!</u>

Suggested Reading: Chapter 9 of Book 'Release the Dove'

Week Four/ Day One

P.U.S.H. (Pray Until Something Happens)

In the labor room on August 3, 2005, Olivier Paul Woodgett entered into this world! One of my best friends Yemisi Adeyemi-Bero who is an IVF (invitro fertilization) specialist, saw his photo and remarked how everything on his body was so "*symmetrical*" in short, he was a perfect baby! Of course, as a 'Glam-ma', I would agree! And....let all the 'Glam-mas' say AMEN!

My daughter had wanted to deliver naturally. Such a wonderful thought! But when Olivier was *non-cooperative*, she decided upon an epidural! Besides, KoKo, (as my grand-son fondly refers to me) had a conference to attend! TD Jakes was hosting a "***Woman Thou Art Loosed***" Conference in Atlanta GA which was 2 hours away. I had friends who had flown internationally to attend this conference. I was on a schedule therefore I began to P.U.S.H in the spirit while my daughter pushed in the natural! Sometimes *pushing* in prayer can seem like child-birth--lengthy, painful and tiresome. Yet at the end, just as Alesea delivered a beautiful, symmetrical son, you too will rejoice and the "labor" (in prayer) would have been well worth it!

Open your Bibles to Matthew 6:5-10

[5] *"When you pray, don't be like the hypocrites who love to pray publicly on street corners and in the synagogues where everyone can see them. I tell you the truth that is all the reward they will ever get.* [6] *But when you pray, go away by yourself, shut the door behind you, and pray to your Father in private. Then your Father, who sees everything, will reward you.*

[7] *"When you pray, don't babble on and on as the Gentiles do. They think their prayers are answered merely by repeating their words again and again.* [8] *Don't be like them, for your Father knows exactly what you need even before you ask him!* [9] *Pray like this:*

Our Father in heaven,
  may your name be kept holy.
[10] *May your Kingdom come soon.*
May your will be done on earth,
as it is in heaven.

Notice verse 10 talks about the will of God. When we pray in every situation, we must know what God's will is. In chapter *5 of "Release the Dove" on page 34,* I give my account on how the Lord revealed his will to me. As I sit writing NOW at nearly 5 a.m. in the morning from Holland, it has just dawned on me that it is absolutely "coincidental" on *MY PART* that I spoke about this in **<u>Chapter 5 on page 34 of *Release the Dove* book!</u>** Gives me goose bumps! That's the verse! **Mark 5:34** and God's will for Olivier! Beloved, I'm just *NOT* that clever! And it's at the top of page 34!!! I'm getting a Holy Ghost Rush y'all!

In America, when my Pastor held my A4 manuscript in his hands, he suggested printing it in the exact same A4 format! Well for now, and for my Oasis Bible Study ladies, that's decided! Whatever happens when it is reprinted, let it be documented that I got this revelation today on October 9, 2016 at 5 a.m.! You might ask why this is so important. Why am I making such a big deal out of this? Because that's exactly how our God speaks!

"But God chose the foolish things of the world to shame the wise; God chose the weak things of the world to shame the strong." 1 Corinthians 1:27.

The most foolish thing I can think of in the Bible is when a prophet would NOT listen to God, God used a donkey to speak to Balaam, *"Then the LORD gave the donkey the ability to speak. "What have I done to you that deserves your beating me three times?" it asked Balaam,"* Numbers 22:28.

In the story of Jonah, he caused a whale to swallow Jonah and then vomit him out so he would obey the Lord! Jonah 1:17.

What do you recall as the most 'foolish' thing you have come across in the Bible? Beloved, remember what you may think is ridiculously foolish and out of this world is actually a '*God Thing'*. Be honest recording your thoughts here.

_____

_____

_____

The Savior of ALL HUMANITY, the King of Kings, Lord of Lords, The I am that I am, Alpha and Omega, First and Last, Ancient of days, The Rock of Ages, Rose of Sharon, Lily of the valley, Balm in Gilead, Jehovah Rapha, Elohim, Me Kadesh, Tsidkenu, Nissi, Roe, El Elyon, my Shield Buckler, Strong Tower, True and Faithful, Bread for the hungry, Water for the thirsty, Husband for the Widow, Father to the Fatherless -------If God Almighty Chose to send His son through a Virgin to be born in a stable-------then I chose to believe He spoke His will to me via a clock's dial and also confirmed it once again just now in **Chapter 5 on page 34 of *Release the Dove* book!!!!** Yes, God does choose the foolish things to confound the wise. If you are sincerely seeking His will, be ready to find it in the most obscure and "un thought of places". Be prepared to think completely *OUT OF THE BOX*. This **IS NOT IN MY OUT-LINE**, but once again I believe it's a God Thing, it's a set up!

Dear hearts, God would like you to know that He still works in mysterious ways. If you seek God's will, you'll find it, but be ready to find it in the unconventional!

Once in ministry, I was at a women's conference and the Lord showed me a particular lady to pray for. Unbeknownst to me at the time, this woman had a long history of infertility but the Lord said that night ended her captivity! After over 15 years of marriage, she had never even experienced a late menstrual cycle! She was 49 years old. The Lord revealed to me, I was to take up her case and He would do the rest. She came to sojourn with me for a period of time after intense prayer, we went to see the doctor together and left rejoicing! *He settles the childless woman in her home as a happy mother of children. Praise the LORD. Psalms 113.9*

Are you experiencing problems of infertility or know someone who is? If you have anointing oil available, anoint yourself right now. This is an act of faith. Place your hands on your womb (or if you are praying for someone else, call out their name), *Lord we curse the spirit of infertility in (name) _____ in the Mighty Name of Jesus. We declare (name) _____ fruitful. Lord as you ended Hannah's barrenness (1 Samuel 1:20), mine (name the person) _____ has also ended* **today***! As Sarah had cause to laugh when she bore Isaiah at a ripe old age (Genesis 21:2), I (_____) too shall have reason to rejoice. Thank you Lord because* **today** *you have turned my mourning into dancing,* **today** *you have turned my captivity as you did with Zion (Psalms 126.1), in the Matchless Name of Jesus we have prayed. Amen.*

Which word used thrice in this prayer indicates **Faith is Now** _____? Correct, then **today** do something **now** to activate your faith!

Take a moment to reflect on a time in your life where God showed up for you in the "strangest most provincial of ways" totally unexpected by you. Be prepared if you like, to share this with the group for edification purposes. Use more space on a separate sheet if you need to. Guess what? Yep. It's now 5:34 a.m.

_____

_____

_____

_____

_____

_____

_____

_____

_____

Session 4: How to pray right, not amiss and pray effective

Week Four/ Day Two

Keys to the Kingdom – First Key – Bind/Forbid

Now turn to Matthew 16:19 NIV

It reads, *"I will give you the **keys** of the kingdom of heaven; whatever you bind on earth will be bound in heaven, and whatever you loose on earth will be loosed in heaven."*

For further clarity, read it in The New Living Translation
*"And I will give you the **keys** of the Kingdom of Heaven. Whatever you forbid on earth will be forbidden in heaven, and whatever you permit on earth will be permitted in heaven."*

What does a key do? You are quite right. Keys unlock doors. When we pray for sickness, financial issues, fruit of the womb, job issues ---these are all doors!

In prayer we are able to speak to these doors,

Psalm 24:9-10 Amplified Bible (AMP)
9

Lift up your heads, O gates,
And lift them up, ancient doors,
That the King of glory may come in.
10

Who is [He then] this King of glory?
The LORD of hosts,
He is the King of glory [who rules over all creation with His heavenly armies]. Selah.

Remember I mentioned to you earlier that the name of Jesus is the same as The Word of God in John 1.1. When we speak a WORD, the will of God in a situation, it will change! The Psalmist says, Lift up your heads, O gates and lift them up, _____.

An *ancient* door signifies a problem might have been there for a very long time but when God speaks life into that problem, that door must open! In other words solutions must come! Situations must be resolved.

List "**Gates or ancient doors**" that need to be addressed in your life or the ones of your loved ones. Then research scriptures that indicate what the *will of God* is in each situation. God's Will is revealed in Scripture in his Word. The Bible says in ***2 Timothy 3:16-17 Amplified Bible (AMP)***

[16] *All Scripture is God-breathed [given by divine inspiration] and is profitable for instruction, for conviction [of sin], for correction [of error and restoration to obedience], for training in righteousness [learning to live in conformity to God's will, both publicly and privately—behaving honorably with personal integrity and moral courage];* [17] *so that the[a] man of God may be complete and proficient, outfitted and thoroughly equipped for every good work.*

An example has been done for you.

Gates or ancient doors (sickness, problems, issues)	Scriptures indicating God's Will in this situation
1. Insomnia	Proverbs 3:24 - When you lie down, you will not be afraid; when you lie down, your sleep will be sweet.

Session 4 - How to Pray Right, not Amiss and Pray Effective

Week Four/ Day Three

Keys to the Kingdom – Second Key – Prayer of Agreement

Later on in Matthew 18:18-19 NIV Jesus gives us a **Second Key**: The prayer of **Agreement.**

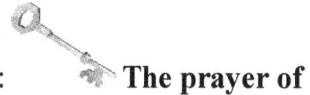

[18] *"Truly I tell you, whatever you bind on earth will be[a] bound in heaven, and whatever you loose on earth will be[b] loosed in heaven.*

[19] *"Again, truly I tell you that if two of you on earth agree about anything they ask for, it will be done for them by my Father in heaven.*

Now read it in the New Living Translation (NLT)

[18] *"I tell you the truth, whatever you forbid[a] on earth will be forbidden in heaven, and whatever you permit[b] on earth will be permitted in heaven.*

[19] *"I also tell you this: If two of you agree here on earth concerning anything you ask, my Father in heaven will do it for you.*

The Prayer of agreement is our second key to unlock spiritual ancient doors and gates. When I first became a born again Christian at the tender age of 19, this is one of the prayers that I used the most! I prayed and agreed with a prayer partner about purchasing a sports car and God did the impossible! I prayed about whether to move to Africa using the prayer of agreement, and the Lord answered! I can go on and on listing answered prayers. As I got older and life was about more than just material things, I learned to fine-tune this wonderful prayer tool.

I cannot stress the importance of having a reliable, confidential prayer partner. As aforementioned, if you are married, your spouse should be the one you pray this type of prayer with. The Bible says in 1 Peter 3:7 *"In the same way, you husbands must give honor to your wives. Treat your wife with understanding as you live together. She may be weaker than you are, but she is your equal partner in God's gift of new life. Treat her as you should so your prayers will not be hindered."*

Please write a definition for the word hindered: _____

According to google dictionary, hinder means to make it difficult for (someone) to do something or for (something) to happen.

We have already established that to get our prayers answered we sometimes need to P.U.S.H. in prayer. P.U.S.H. is the acronym for _____.

After laboring in prayer, you certainly do not want any hindrances to take place. You don't want ANYTHING or ANYBODY to cause your prayer to fail.
Now write a few Synonyms for hinder : hamper, be a hindrance ,_____ ,
_____to thwart, _____ ,
_____ , forestall, _____ , slow down,
set back.

I don't believe anyone reading this would want their prayers to be hindered. What are some other causes of our prayers being hindered?

1. _ _ _ _ _ t
2. u_ _ _ l _ _ _
3. _ n _ _ _ _ _ v _ _ s_

I call those the triplets of blessing blockers. These conditions can literally keep you from receiving the blessings God has already proposed for you.

Another hindrance to our prayers can simply be the influence of Satan and his cohorts.

Please read Ephesians 6:10-20 in the Amplified. To see this verse better, I would like for you to underline WHO our struggle is really against. Next high-light everything about this scripture that refers to a soldier. Afterwards, using the soldier drawing, write out the spiritual parts of our armor (*Image: Free Pinterest drawing 389 x774*).

The Armor of God

[10] *In conclusion, be strong in the Lord [draw your strength from Him and be empowered through your union with Him] and in the power of His [boundless] might.* [11] *Put on the full armor of God [for His precepts are like the splendid armor of a heavily-armed soldier], so that you may be able to [successfully] stand up against all the schemes and the strategies and the deceits of the devil.* [12] *For our struggle is not against flesh and blood [contending only with physical opponents], but against the rulers, against the powers, against the world forces of this [present] darkness, against the spiritual forces of wickedness in the heavenly (supernatural) places.* [13] *Therefore, put on the complete armor of God, so that you will be able to [successfully] resist and stand your ground in the evil day [of danger], and having done everything [that the crisis demands], to stand firm [in your place, fully prepared, immovable, victorious].* [14] *So stand firm and hold your ground, HAVING [a]TIGHTENED THE WIDE BAND OF TRUTH (personal integrity, moral courage) AROUND YOUR WAIST and HAVING PUT ON THE BREASTPLATE OF RIGHTEOUSNESS (an upright heart),* [15] *and having [b]strapped on YOUR FEET THE*

GOSPEL OF PEACE IN PREPARATION [to face the enemy with firm-footed stability and the readiness produced by the good news]. ¹⁶ *Above all, lift up the [protective]* ^[c]*shield of faith with which you can extinguish all the flaming arrows of the evil one.* ¹⁷ *And take* THE HELMET OF SALVATION, *and the sword of the Spirit, which is the Word of God.*

¹⁸ *With all prayer and petition pray [with specific requests] at all times [on every occasion and in every season] in the Spirit, and with this in view, stay alert with all perseverance and petition [interceding in prayer] for all* ^[d]*God's people.* ¹⁹ *And pray for me, that words may be given to me when I open my mouth, to proclaim boldly the mystery of the good news [of salvation],* ²⁰ *for which I am an ambassador in chains. And pray that in proclaiming it I may speak boldly and courageously, as I should.*

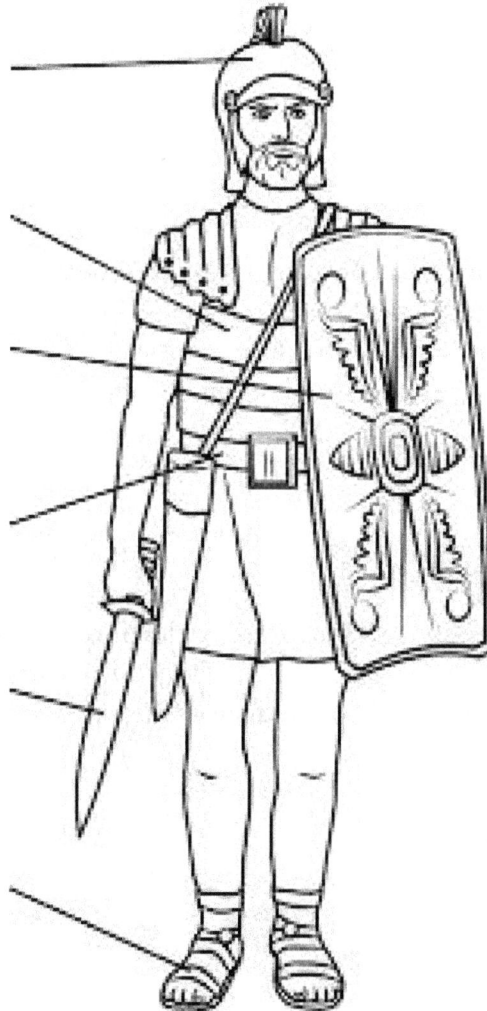

Growing up in my Church in Alabama, this is a song that we used to sing. I sang it with enthusiasm and vivacity not fully understanding what it meant until I truly joined the ranks of a fighting soldier in God's army!

By: Lyle Lovett

I'm a soldier in the army of the Lord

I'm a soldier in the army of the Lord
I'm a soldier in the army
I'm a soldier in the army of the Lord
I'm a soldier in the army

I'm a soldier in the army of the Lord
I'm a soldier in the army
I'm a soldier in the army of the Lord
I'm a soldier in the army

I got my war clothes on in the army of the Lord
I got my war clothes on in the army
I got my war clothes on in the army of the Lord
I got my war clothes on in the army

I'm a soldier in the army of the Lord
I'm a soldier in the army

I'm a soldier in the army of the Lord
I'm a soldier in the army

I believe I'll die in the army of the Lord
I believe I'll die in the army
I believe I'll die in the army of the Lord
I believe I'll die in the army

I'm a soldier in the army of the Lord
I'm a soldier in the army
I'm a soldier in the army of the Lord
I'm a soldier in the army

I got my breastplate on in the army of the Lord
Got my breastplate on in the army
I got my breastplate on in the army of the Lord
I got my breastplate on in the army

Repeat Chorus

Most likely if you are a woman, you could have easily identified with my illustration of the labor room in the spirit and how to **PUSH** (Pray until something happens). But have you ever thought about the fact that we are constantly in warfare and it is NOT against flesh and blood (Ephesians 6:12)? You cannot see our opponent but God can. There is an invisible army that is protecting you at all times.

PRAYER TIME!

If you don't have a prayer partner, ask the Lord to show you whom this person should be. Ideally, the person should be trustworthy, confidential and a believer. Write down a prayer request. There might be ancient doors involved, write those down. Now using the keys above—pray a prayer of agreement—address that issue with your prayer partner. For these type of prayers, practice praying out loud. If you are not accustomed to, help is on the way!

Use the space below:

Session 4: How to Pray Right, not Amiss and Pray Effective

Week Four/ Day Four

Keys to the Kingdom – Third Key - Angels

On Page 57 you completed an exercise regarding gates in your lives with scriptures next to each gate. In your small groups, break into partners of 2, take one ancient existing door or gate, using the 3 keys, command that gate to be lifted up! Each partner prays for each other. Pray Right, not Amis. Watch the angels harvest your prayers

Look back to Psalms 24:9-10, the scripture reads *'who is [He then] this King of glory?*
The L*ORD of hosts, He is the King of glory [**who rules over all creation with His heavenly armies**]. Selah.*

Verse 10 says *He* speaking of Jesus, rules over all creation with His heavenly armies! Dearly, beloved we are in the army of the Lord! When did you enroll? You signed up when you accepted Jesus Christ as Lord and Savior! You were automatically enlisted. When you accept God's gift of salvation you automatically inherit Eternal life and you have access to God's military. If you are curious about the Lord's heavenly army, flip in your Bible to 2 Kings 6:15-17Amplified Bible (AMP)

15 The servant of the man of God got up early and went out, and behold, there was an army with horses and chariots encircling the city. Elisha's servant said to him, "Oh no, my master! What are we to do?" 16 Elisha answered, "Do not be afraid, for those who are with us are more than those who are with them." 17 Then Elisha prayed and said, "LORD, please, open his eyes that he may see." And the LORD opened the servant's eyes and he saw; and behold, the mountain was full of horses and chariots of fire surrounding Elisha.

Angels are at our disposition to bring about God's will upon this earth. This brings me to my third key. Look in Hebrews 1:13. This book talks about the supremacy of Christ. It defines what angels are and what their roles are.

*'To which of his angels did God ever say, sit at my right hand until I make your enemies a footstool for your feet. Are not **all angels ministering spirits** sent to **serve those who will** inherit*

salvation?' Who are those? US!!! Right answer! Angels are

_____ sent to _____ .

Angels are the 3rd Key at our disposition to lift and remove ancient doors and gates! As we pray on earth, bind problems of sickness, finances, fruit of the womb, and release healing using scripture from Isaiah 53:5, angels take those scriptures, those words past the principalities of evil in high places straight to Jesus. Where is Jesus sat? On the right hand of the Father. Jesus takes those prayers to the Father because He lives to intercede for us.

Hebrews 7:25. I was listening to Ron Carpenter's series on "Armored" and it was very enlightening regarding the role of angels upon the earth.

Angels ONLY HEARKEN TO SCRIPTURE, THE WORD OF GOD.

They do not obey when we murmur and complain. Only speaking the Word of God moves them on our behalf!

Daniel 10 gives a wonderful illustration of how Daniel had prayed and fasted for 21 days. After 21 days, Michael, the angel of God came to give Daniel a startling message! He told him that from the moment he prayed his prayers reached the heavens but the prince of Persia came to block his prayer. Remember Ephesians 6:12 says our warfare is NOT against flesh and blood but _____

_____ in heavenly realms.

The evil spirit (s) of the Prince of Persia detained Daniel for 21 days, but because Daniel persevered in prayer, the angel also persevered and came to Daniel's rescue. That is a magnificent illustration of how our prayers might be hindered. That the principalities of the air may prevent our answers from coming. But when you bind, loose and agree upon the Word of God, you are bound to get your solution!

In Ron Carpenter's Armored series says many complain and gripe with much negativity. Angels do not move to our emotions. Only when the Word of God is spoken in faith. Angels reap the harvest **Matthew 13:37-42 9 Read**. They are sitting and waiting for harvest but no seed has gone out! Seed is the Word of God which you must speak in order to bring about a harvest.

When Olivier was ill, I constantly looked to the hills from whence cometh my help! **Psalms 121**. I determined from the start that my help would come from the Lord not doctors. The Lord had shown me in **Mark 5:34** that it would be my faith that would bring about Olivier's healing. It was my job to PUSH in the spirit until I got relief!

Beloved, let me reiterate this fact: we do not need to pray for healing, God has already given us our healing. When you are a born again Christian, divine healing is a benefit! We only need to claim it and receive it.

We have covered much today. Let's do a quick recap. Write the three keys that I mentioned in receiving our healing or answers to prayers.

1.

2.

3.

What did the above reading from Daniel prove to you concerning the importance of persevering in prayer?

Do you remember a time that you were about to give up on God regarding a certain prayer request then suddenly an answer came through?   If yes, discuss that experience here.

Why do you think that particular prayer was hindered?

Can you imagine the magnitude of warfare that might have taken place in the heavenlies just to bring about your request?

Do you think the Lord sent an angel to release your blessing?

Why or why not?

Nuggets Gleaned from Today's Study:

+

+

+

Session 4: How to Pray Right, not Amiss and Pray effectively

Week Four/ Day Five

Christian Soldier! Take up your stand and claim what is rightfully yours!

The Bible refers to Jesus as a Mediator, Priest & Advocate. Notice these are legal terms. He was announced by Isaiah in a different light in 9:5-6. Not as a religious man but as a political man.

For every boot of the marching warrior in the battle tumult,
And [every soldier's] garment rolled in blood, will be used for burning, fuel for the fire.
6

For to us a Child shall be born, to us a Son shall be given;
And the government shall be upon His shoulder,
And His name shall be called Wonderful Counselor, Mighty God,
Everlasting Father, Prince of Peace.

Christian soldier, do you see your role a little bit differently now? Can you see that Jesus is The King of Kings and Lord of Lords? In our spiritual warfare, not only do we take up spiritual garments but we also have the power to exercise our God given rights to execute the will of God upon this earth. **1 John 5**:14 *"This is the confidence we have in approaching God; THAT IF WE ASK ANYTHING ACCORDING TO HIS WILL, HE HEARS US. (emphasis mine) 15 And if we know that he hears us—whatever we ask—we know that we have what we asked of him.*

If I ask anything according to his will, He will do it. The Old Testament Priest would take the sins of the people into the temple once a year. But Jesus is the New Testament priest according to Hebrews 12:24. He is the mediator of the new covenant.

> Jesus is not bound to fulfill promises He didn't make. If He made it and you are saved, you have access.
>
> (Ron Carpenter, Armored)

Jesus takes our prayers and negotiates with the Father, He is a mediator, to the Father. He is a High Priest. Now as a believer, you can approach the throne of grace with assurance. *"So let us come boldly to the throne of our gracious God. There we will receive his mercy, and we will find grace to help us when we need it most."* Hebrews 4:16

Let's recap what we have learned.

How often did the Old Testament priests take the sins of the people into the temple_____?

How many times did Jesus take the sins of the people into the temple? _____?
Which scripture tells you that? _____.

Jesus is a _____ of the new covenant.

These legal terms have been used to describe Jesus.

    a._____

    b._____

    c._____

The Bible says in Isaiah 9:6 the _____ is upon his shoulders. What does that mean to you during these trying times we are experiencing in the world today? _____ _____ Which scripture in the Bible tells us to pray for our government officials and leaders? _____.

Jesus, the Example: Hebrews Chapter 12

12 Therefore, since we are surrounded by so great a cloud of[a]witnesses [who by faith have testified to the truth of God's absolute faithfulness], stripping off every unnecessary weight and the sin which so easily and cleverly entangles us, let us run with endurance and active persistence the race that is set before us, 2 [looking away from all that will distract us and] focusing our eyes on Jesus, who is the Author and Perfecter of faith [the first incentive for our belief and the One who brings our faith to maturity], who for the joy [of accomplishing the goal] set before Him endured the cross, [b]disregarding the shame, and sat down at the right hand of the throne of God [revealing His deity, His authority, and the completion of His work].

3 Just consider and meditate on Him who endured from sinners such bitter hostility against Himself [consider it all in comparison with your trials], so that you will not grow weary and lose heart.

Skip to verse 12

12 So then, strengthen hands that are weak and knees that tremble. 13 Cut through and make smooth, straight paths for your feet [that are safe and go in the right direction], so that the leg which is lame may not be put out of joint, but rather may be healed.

> Do not wait on heaven. Heaven is waiting on earth. We are waiting for God to do something. Use your key, doors will open.

Skip to verse 22

22 But you have come to Mount Zion and to the city of the living God, the heavenly Jerusalem, and to myriads of angels [in festive gathering], 23 and to the general assembly and assembly of the firstborn who are registered [as citizens] in heaven, and to God, who is Judge of all, and to the spirits of the righteous (the redeemed in heaven) who have been made perfect [bringing them to their final glory], 24 and to Jesus, the Mediator of a new covenant [uniting God and man], and to the sprinkled blood, which speaks [of mercy], a better and nobler and more gracious message than the blood of Abel [which cried out for vengeance].

> Discuss **WHO** are the great cloud of witnesses in verse 12 of the previous reading. Use New Testament scripture to back up your response.

> *Stripping off all necessary weight and the sin that so easily entangles us refers to the need of _____. Who is the only one who can do that for you? _____. Please research what that name is in the Hebrew language. _____.*

You will recall in the previous chapter, we had an in-depth discussion of Ephesians 6:10-20. We broached upon the topic of your being a soldier in the army of the Lord. I would now like to show you through the Illustration drawn by my daughter Danielle for our Oasis Bible Ladies study in Kuala Lumpur Malaysia around 2009 or 10. So engrossed was I in intercession that I wanted the Oasis women to understand their elevated position in Christ. This poster today still serves as a visual which I use in teaching effective intercession as well as standing in the gap for a loved one.

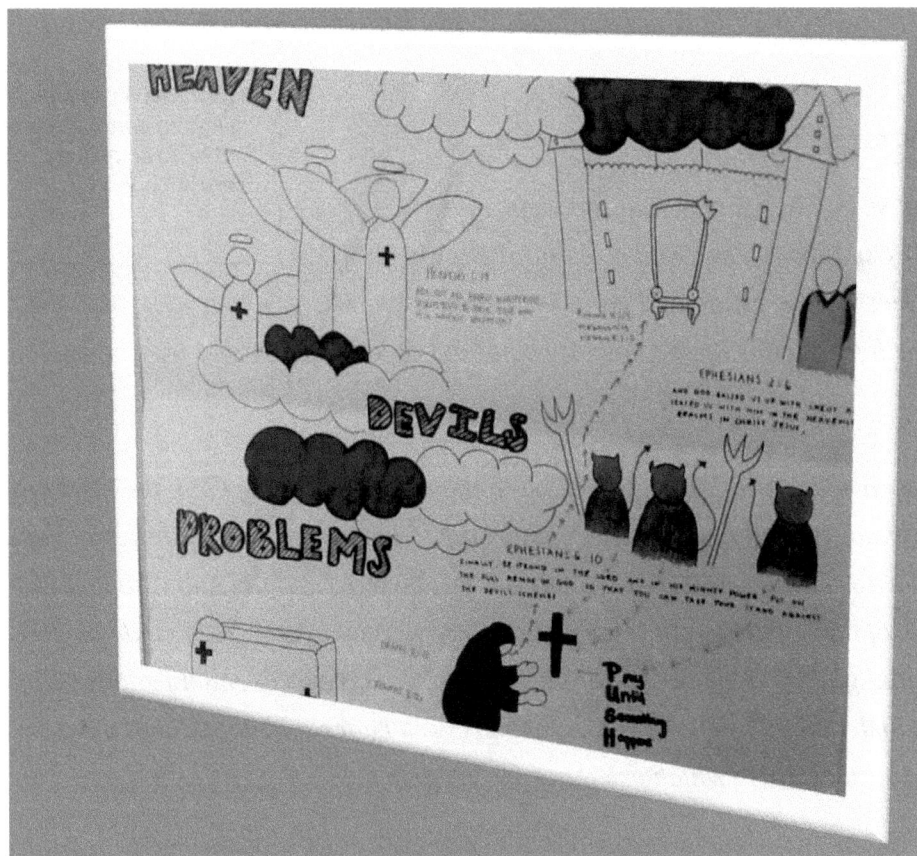

Do you remember how many days Daniel (Daniel chapter 10) prayed before his solution arrived? _____. Why was Daniel's prayer hindered?
_____.

What do we need to do in order to get solutions to our prayers? Discuss in your small groups. How I would love to be there listening to the clamor of coffee cups and lively conversation going on right about now.

1._____

2._____

3._____

4._____

5._____

Please recall an answered prayer that you have had in your life. What was the situation and how did God come to your rescue? Were there any hindrances? How long did it take from the moment you began to pray until the answer arrived? Imagine the spiritual warfare that most likely took place in the heaven-lies, don't you feel blessed right about now!

_____
_____
_____
_____
_____
_____
_____
_____
_____

Take a short breather! Complete the puzzle from memory of what you know

About Ephesians 6 (*Penterest free image*).

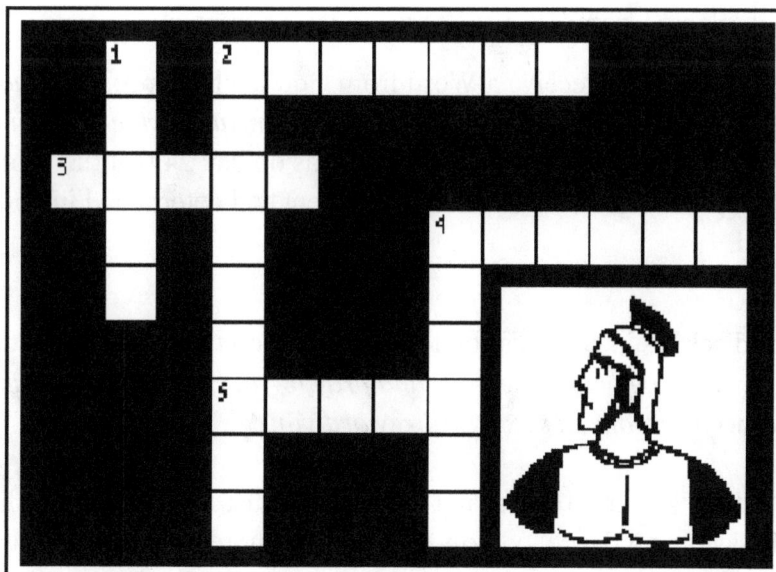

Session 5: How I took authority over Olivier's illness, and obtained his healing through Faith

Suggested Reading: Chapters 10-14 of Book 'Release the Dove'

Week Five/ Day One

Easter Sunday 2015

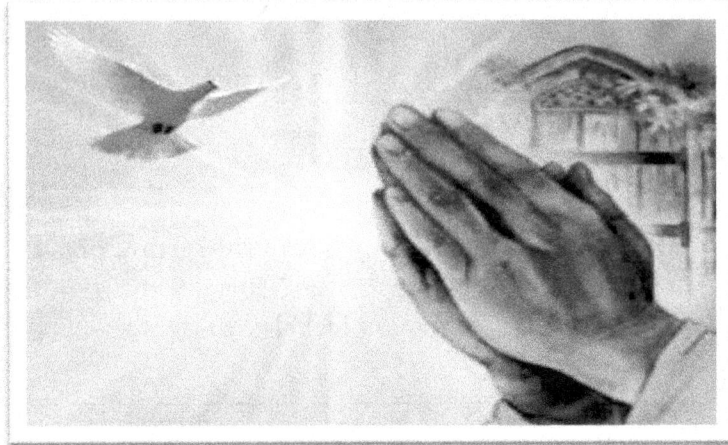

Image by Pinterest 464 x 412

Preparation for Easter Sunday is always a special time for me as I am sure it is for most believing Christians. I usually fast before this event and this year I had declared a *"Word Fast"* although I also fasted food, my desire was to be inundated and saturated to the overflow in God's Word.

A fast in the 'religious sense' is to abstain from food. In order to understand my *'Word Fast'* you must look at it differently. Think of it as a proclamation. Often in the Word of God, we see fasts being proclaimed. As in Jonah when he was sanctioned to go to the Nineveh and proclaim the Word of God. The King himself came down from his throne and proclaimed a fast. The Ninevites from the least to the greatest, even the animals fasted. The Lord saw the hearts of these people and relented from His plans to destroy that great city.

The prophet Daniel fasted to receive a Word from God in chapter 3:2, '*In those days I, Daniel, was mourning for three weeks. [3] I ate no delicacies, no meat or wine entered my mouth, nor did I anoint myself at all, for the full three weeks.*' It was on day 24 that the Word of God came with great power through an angel! You must be persistent and determined in your fasting to receive a Word from God.

Jesus said to his disciples in continuation to the sermon on the mount in Matthew 6.6, *"But when you pray go into your room close the door and pray to your Father who is unseen, Then your Father who sees what is done in secret will reward you."*

Therefore my fast for Easter 2015 was not primarily to fast food but also to fast my words to hear God's. My fast was a desire to know God's Word more and more. To go into my closet and be silent while God spoke. I set my face like flint to hear from God and Him only. This is what I meant by a Word fast. Ezekiel 3:3 says, *Then he said to me, "Son of man, eat this scroll I am giving you and fill your stomach with it." So I ate it, and it tasted as sweet as honey in my mouth."* I suppose in essence that is what I did.

Psalms 119:103 exclaims, *"How sweet are Your words to my taste! Yes, sweeter than honey to my mouth!"*

And again in Jeremiah 15:16, *"Your words were found and I ate them, And Your words became for me a joy and the delight of my heart; For I have been called by Your name, O LORD God of hosts.*

I cannot stress enough the importance God's Word in healing. All of Olivier's healing hinged on the Word in Mark 5. When I spoke to the doctors, I was motivated by the Word of God. His Word became my bread and water. So my Word fast was an extended time to hear from God's Word, speak it back to the doctors and the people around me and watch his Word unfold and be fulfilled.

Clement and I had attended Good Friday Service with our hosts Shereen and William at their Church during that time.

All week long, I had been discussing with Olivier's team of neurologists about removing his life support and taking him off unnecessary medication. I related to you earlier how the Lord had revealed to me via *'a clock dial'* to read Mark 5:34 that it would be through my faith that Olivier would be healed. The Lord had also shown me that the medication he was taking was the cause of his health degradation. Yet, my getting that across to his well-organized team of neurologists was a different story. They were busy being efficient, sending important tests to England, awaiting results at month's end. Believe me, they were doing all of the natural things that a reputable hospital would have done! They were caring and attentive. They were doing all within their power to get Olivier well. Yet the Bible says, *"For the wisdom of this world is foolishness to God. As the Scriptures say, "He traps the wise in the snare of their own cleverness."* 1 Corinthians 3:19.

This is where I believe when man's strength ends, the Lord's begin. All of the wisdom of the earth is less than 0 in light of our God's wisdom. He is the greatest physician! Having made all the delicate, inner parts of Olivier's body and knit them together in his mother's womb. (Psalms 139:13) I knew Olivier's healing would manifest.

In Genesis 2:7 it states, *"Then the LORD God formed the man from the dust of the ground. He breathed the breath of life into the man's nostrils, and the man became a living person."* This indicated to me that Olivier did not need life support to breath. God was more than capable to breathe life back into his lungs.

It might seem as if someone like me who had studied in the health field would not think on such a *simple level.* But the Lord said we need to come as little children unto him.

Research the New International Standard version of Matthew 18:3 and write what it says.

Then he said, "I tell all of you with certainty, unless you _____,
_____ you will never get into the kingdom from heaven.

The Lord would have us come to him as little children. When my grand-daughter saw her recovering brother, she could hardly talk but these words she uttered matter-of-factly, "You are going to be all right Olivier". Now that's faith in action!

What does the Kingdom of heaven consists of according to Romans 14:17?

"¹⁷ For the kingdom of God is not a matter of _____ and _____ but of
_____ and _____ and _____ in the Holy Spirit."

The Lord also wanted me to see that all of my ceremonial fasting worrying what I should and should not eat during this fast was a fiasco! Instead the Lord wanted me to experience His type of fast which is righteousness, peace and joy in the Holy Spirit! Although this was not a "joyful time" in the human sense but in the spiritual it was! For no other time in my life had I experienced such intimacy and closeness with the Lord.

Session 5: How I took authority over Olivier's illness and obtained his healing through faith

Week Five/ Day Two

Acceptable Fast of the Lord

Let's look at what the Lord revealed to me in my early days in the 90's when I was newly learning to fast and to hear His voice. I lived in The Congo at the time. I had adapted to a life-style of fasting and prayer. I learned how to intercede in wee the hours of the night. On this particular occasion, the Holy Spirit revealed to me God's type of fast!

I had been fasting food for days, immersed in prayer. I was an ESL (English as a Second Language) instructor for various Petroleum companies in the area. I went briefly to the office to make copies for my students. While there, one of the young ladies vexed me to no end. My fleshly emotions rose up in me! Hungry, tired and feeling justified, I laid into her, 'sparing nary a word!' May I also mention, she was a sister in Christ? Though I might have felt justified, the Holy Spirit let me know that my actions WERE NOT justified! Clearly, I heard the Spirit of the Lord saying to me to go home. I obeyed! Arriving in my home, I went to my bedroom and began to lament. The Lord ordered me to be quiet and lay prostrate on the floor and listen! I heard him say to read Isaiah 58.

Observances of Fasts

58 "Cry aloud, do not hold back;

Lift up your voice like a trumpet,

and declare to My people their transgression

And to the house of Jacob their sins.

2

"Yet they seek Me day by day and delight [superficially] to know My ways,

As [if they were in reality] a nation that has done righteousness

And has not abandoned (turned away from) the ordinance of their God.

They ask of Me righteous judgments,

They delight in the nearness of God.

3

'Why have we fasted,' they say, 'and You do not see it?

Why have we humbled ourselves and You do not notice?'

Hear this [O Israel], on the day of your fast [when you should be grieving for your sins] you find something you desire [to do],

And you force your hired servants to work [instead of stopping all work, as the law teaches].

4

"The facts are that you fast only for strife and brawling and to strike with the fist of wickedness.

You do not fast as you do today to make your voice heard on high.
5

"Is a fast such as this what I have chosen, a day for a man to humble himself [with sorrow in his soul]?
Is it only to bow down his head like a reed
And to make sackcloth and ashes as a bed [pretending to have a repentant heart]?
Do you call this a fast and a day pleasing to the LORD?
6

"[Rather] is this not the fast which I choose,
To undo the bonds of wickedness,
To tear to pieces the ropes of the yoke,
To let the oppressed go free
And break apart every [enslaving] yoke?
"Is it not to divide your bread with the hungry
And bring the homeless poor into the house;
When you see the naked, that you cover him,
And not to hide yourself from [the needs of] your own flesh and blood?
8

"Then your light will break out like the dawn,
And your healing (restoration, new life) will quickly spring forth;
Your righteousness will go before you [leading you to peace and prosperity],
The glory of the LORD will be your rear guard.
9

"Then you will call, and the LORD will answer;
You will cry for help, and He will say, 'Here I am.'
If you take away from your midst the yoke [of oppression],
The finger pointed in scorn [toward the oppressed or the godly], and [every form of] wicked (sinful, unjust) speech,
10

And if you offer yourself to [assist] the hungry
And satisfy the [a]need of the afflicted,
Then your light will rise in darkness
And your gloom will become like midday.
11

""And the LORD will continually guide you,
And satisfy your soul in scorched and dry places,

74

And give strength to your bones;

And you will be like a watered garden,

And like a spring of water whose waters do not fail.

12

"And your people will rebuild the ancient ruins;

You will raise up and restore the age-old foundations [of buildings that have been laid waste];

You will be called Repairer of the Breach,

Restorer Keeping the Sabbath

13

"If you turn back your foot from [[c]unnecessary travel on] the Sabbath,

From doing your own pleasure on My holy day,

And call the Sabbath a [spiritual] delight, and the holy day of the LORD honorable,

And honor it, not going your own way

Or [d]engaging in your own pleasure

Or speaking your own [idle] words,

14

Then you will take pleasure in the LORD,

And

I will make you ride on the high places of the earth,

And I will feed you with the [promised] heritage of Jacob your father;

For the mouth of the LORD has spoken."

Questions for Reflection

1). In the episode I have just relayed to you regarding a day of fasting in The Congo, which verse in Isaiah 58 do you think the Lord used to speak directly to my situation?

2). In Olivier's situation, which verse in Isaiah 58 do you think the Lord used to speak directly to my situation and why?   Write out the verse of scripture here.

3). How do you lose cords of injustice in the Spirit? Be pensive. Use learned scripture.

4). How do you lose cords of injustice in the natural? Be practical.

5). Have you ever fasted food for spiritual reasons?　　　If yes, reflect on one of these occasions. How did your fast mostly resemble Isaiah 58?

What does fasting actually do for you as a physical and spiritual being?

Use a scale from 1-10. Ten being the highest reflection of Isaiah 58.

   a. My fast ended in strife and arguing.　　　　　　＿＿＿＿＿

   b. My fast involved me helping the poor　　　　　　＿＿＿＿＿

   c. My fast helped the oppressed to go free　　　　　＿＿＿＿＿

   d. My fast helped prisoners go free　　　　　　　　＿＿＿＿＿

   e. On the day of my fast, I enjoy the spa　　　　　＿＿＿＿＿

   f. On the day of my fast, I read God's Word　　　　＿＿＿＿＿

   g. On the day of my fast, I enjoy my favorite desert　＿＿＿＿＿

                          Total　　＿＿＿＿＿

Add up your score and reflect on how you can better improve 'your fast'.

The above account of my first experience with Isaiah 58 while fasting is one of the most humbling experiences I have ever had in my life. I learned to abide by his Word:

1 Peter 5:6-9 Amplified Bible (AMP)

[6] Therefore humble yourselves under the mighty hand of God [set aside self-righteous pride], so that He may exalt you [to a place of honor in His service] at the appropriate time, [7] casting all your cares [all your anxieties, all your worries, and all your concerns, once and for all] on Him, for He cares about you [with deepest affection, and watches over you very carefully]. [8] Be sober [well balanced and self-disciplined], be alert and cautious at all times. That enemy of yours, the devil, prowls around like a roaring lion [fiercely hungry], seeking someone to devour. [9] But resist him, be firm in your faith [against his attack—rooted, established, immovable], knowing that the same experiences of suffering are being experienced by your brothers and sisters throughout the world. [You do not suffer alone.

Take some time out to pray and ask the Lord to humble you as you pray or fast or seek His face. Try to remember, it is all about Him, you will gain much in the process, I promise you! Remember Jesus had to go through Golgotha before dying on the cross. There is a 'stripping away' of self which is necessary to truly be of service to the Master. Tomorrow will be easier as we put on our spiritual armor and march towards victory!

Session 5: How I took authority over Olivier's illness and obtained his healing through faith

Week Five/ Day Three

Commission

WORD TREASURE HUNT: Discuss in your small group *Isaiah 58.* Cross reference it with *Isaiah 61:1-5.* Isaiah prophesied and the Lord fulfilled this prophecy in *Luke 4:18-20.*

The Spirit of the Lord GOD is upon me,
Because the LORD has anointed and commissioned me
To bring good news to the humble and afflicted;
He has sent me to bind up [the wounds of] the brokenhearted,
To proclaim release [from confinement and condemnation] to the [physical and spiritual] captives
And freedom to prisoners,
To proclaim [a]the favorable year of the LORD,
[b]And the day of vengeance and retribution of our God,
To comfort all who mourn,
To grant to those who mourn in Zion the following:
To give them a [c]turban instead of dust [on their heads, a sign of mourning],
The oil of joy instead of mourning,
The garment [expressive] of praise instead of a disheartened spirit.
So they will be called the trees of righteousness [strong and magnificent, distinguished for integrity, justice, and right standing with God],
The planting of the LORD, that He may be glorified
Then they will rebuild the ancient ruins,
They will raise up and restore the former desolations;
And they will renew the ruined cities,
The desolations (deserted settlements) of many generations.
Strangers will stand and feed your flocks,

Who else has God commissioned to 'preach' the gospel? Circle all that applies.

      a. Preachers

      b. Evangelists

      c. Deacons

      d. Elders

      e. Me

How do you know?

Read Luke 10:19, Mark 16.15-20. At which occasion did the Lord Jesus make each commission?

How can YOU 'preach' the gospel or pray for the sick or other issues in your own environment i.e. your home, work, extended family?

I often tell people, we might be the only Bible someone reads.

In the text we just read, what might be the 'good news' we can bring to the humble and afflicted?

Action Project

Look around your neighborhood, your place of business, your church or even on the street. Choose someone this week that you can bring 'good news' to. It might be to prepare a meal for the hungry, babysit for a single Mom, give money to the homeless on the streets or visit the sick in the hospital or prisoners in the penitentiary. There are many who have become prisoners to alcohol, drugs, cigarettes, life-style or bad habits. How might you take the good news to them?

_____

_____

_____

_____

"Since his days are determined, and the number of his months is with you, and you have appointed his limits that he cannot pass," Job 14:5.

I knew Olivier had NOT reached his limit! I had prayed a prayer for him at his birth, dedicated him to God and written a poem (page 4 of *Release the Dove* book), I knew my God could not lie nor go back on his promises.

"God is not a man, so he does not lie. He is not human, so he does not change his mind. Has he ever spoken and failed to act? Has he ever promised and not carried it through? Numbers 23:19.

In the same way, I am relating this story to you, God was speaking to me. Through his Word in a conversational form.

Session 5: How I took authority over Olivier's illness and obtained his healing through faith

Week Five/ Day Three

Peace in the Midst of my Storm

The most incredible thing that I experienced besides the miracle itself was to remain in peace throughout the duration of the illness. Did I sometimes doubt or wonder how God was going to do it? No, I never did. Because of the Word He gave me I knew that He would orchestrate and administer healing just as His Word said.

Isaiah 26:3 reads "He whose mind is stead-fast on me, I will keep in perfect peace."
In another version it reads, "*You keep him in perfect peace whose mind is stayed on you, because he trusts in you. Trust in the LORD forever, for the LORD GOD is an everlasting rock.*"

Think of a rock. I remember in the early years of Oasis, Pam Osterland, our then Prayer Coordinator blessed Oasis with gifts of small rocks with Bible verses written on them. These precious gems could be easily transported in our purses or pockets as a constant reminder of who our Rock truly is! It also served as a fantastic conversational piece!

One of our Oasis ladies went into labor carrying her rock with her the whole while! As she held tight to her rock, she was reminded of who the True Rock is, in fact it was His hand she held and His Word she held fast to.

Look at these Bible verses about our Rock

- 2 Samuel 22:32 *"For who is God, besides the LORD? And who is a rock, besides our God?*

- 1 Samuel 2:2 *"There is no one holy like the LORD, Indeed, there is no one besides You, nor is there any rock like our God.*

- Isaiah 44:8 *'Do not tremble and do not be afraid; have I not long since announced it to you and declared it? And you are My witnesses Is there any God besides Me, Or is there any other Rock? I know of none.'"*

- Psalm 144:1 *Blessed be the LORD, my rock, Who trains my hands for war, And my fingers for battle;*

- Deuteronomy 32:4 *"The Rock! His work is perfect, for all His ways are just; A God of faithfulness and without injustice, Righteous and upright is He.*

- Psalms 71:3 *Be to me a rock of habitation to which I may continually come; You have given commandment to save me, For You are my rock and my fortress.*

ACTIVITY

Perhaps you would like to create your own tangible reminders in the form of *"rocks"* using the scriptures above or others the Lord may give you. These will serve as anchors throughout the storms of life bringing to your remembrance that our True Rock is God! He never fails and He will never let you down.

Who is the One who provides PERFECT Peace? _____. Do you know what God's Hebrew name for peace is? Please research and write it here._____

What definition is given for this name? Complete the sequence.

1- Peace
2- _____
3- _____
4- Prosperity
5- _____

Now from all you've just read, please write your definition of peace

_____

_____

_____

Think of a recent time or perhaps something you are going through right now that warrants an entrance of the Prince of Peace, Jehovah Shalom. Please share (only if you feel led), in your small groups. Did you allow doubt and fear to seep in?

_____

_____

_____

_____

For me, peace is the absence of fear. When our minds are bogged down, worried and concerned about the future, we allow doubt and fear to supersede our faith. When this happens, we lose sight of what God said. The Bible clearly states that a double minded man shall receive nothing from God (James 1:8).

So what should be our focus? God's Word. Not the problem, but what God says about it. Ultimately He will bring all things into perfect synchronization.

So let's review, please recall the Word that the Lord spoke to me using the clock's dial as a sign. Write the verse and scripture here._____

_____

I knew that God was asking me to have faith for Olivier's healing and remain in peace. Fear is the absence of faith. Doubt is the absence of faith.

It was no coincidence that the Lord gave me the theme for the conference that previous year Talitha Cumi Arise!

Read in your Bibles from **Mark 5:34-43.**
All of Olivier's healing hinged on these scriptures. When I arrived at the hospital the morning I had received that Word, Olivier's condition had grown worst. Throughout the entire ordeal, Olivier had been lucid and talking. But that morning, when I spoke to him he acknowledged me but would not open his eyes. The doctors could not rouse him so they sent him immediately to

ICU placing on his body lifesaving paraphernalia i.e. breathing tube, heart monitor along with 24 hour surveillance.

It was God's grace that gave me that Word that morning before arriving at the hospital.

> *My Pastor in Malaysia, Pastor Amos, often says one week away from church makes you weak!*
> *'If thou faint in the day of adversary, your strength is small.'*
> *Proverbs 24:10*

From Mark 5, the Lord showed me these important truths. High-light these scriptures in your Bible:

<u>Write the verse, I'll provide the explanation</u>

Mark 5:26 _____

I knew that I had to get Olivier off of the medicine and breathing machine. We had spent much time and effort going to two different hospitals. We were evacuated from Malaysia to Singapore, which was the 3rd hospital. We had incurred many bills (which were all mostly paid in full thankfully) and had two very large bags of medicine. Yet Olivier was not well. In fact He was worst!

Vs 34: _____

I knew from this key verse that I had to have faith for Olivier's healing. It would be my faith literally which would make him whole.

Vs 39: _____

Although Olivier appeared to be in a coma and wasting away, I knew he would not die but would live! According to this Word he was only sleeping. In fact the Lord did not allow the doctors to even use the word coma. Instead they said he had 'decreased consciousness". So convinced was Olivier's nanny of his eventual healing that she also repeated this same statement to the doctors. Olivier was only sleeping after all he had gone 3 days with no sleep! As the people laughed Jesus to scorn, they also labeled me as someone who was out of touch with reality. And truly I was! The only reality I knew was the reality of God's Word!

Vs 40: _____

When you are going through a crisis, it is very important not to listen to anyone else's logic if it contradicts the Word that the Lord has given you for your particular situation. Like Jesus, he removed every doubter from the room! Now that I had successfully convinced Clement and Rose that Olivier would fully recuperate, I had to get my daughter and son n law also to believe.

Verse
41_____

After returning from the Indian Church on Easter Sunday, I sat at Olivier's bed-side and the Lord instantly starting speaking|:

'Woman of God, do you believe?"
'Yes Lord,' I do believe.
'Speak life!'

I instantly looked at Olivier's lifeless body, stood up and commanded his ears and eyes to open. Commanded him to speak. The Lord had instructed me to read Ezekiel 37 about the Valley of Dry Bones. I knew I had to speak life and I did. Please read Ezekiel 37 in your Bible.

I sat back down and began to sing. '*I believe, yes I receive it. (my healing), I believe yes I receive it, my deliverance.*' I sang this song in Olivier's stead. The words overflowed from my lips out of the depths of my innermost being. As I sang, the nurses came in to suction and do their usual care. I moved out of their way and stood to the side of Olivier's bed. As the nurse suctioned, Olivier started coughing! I started praising God! This was the first reaction we had gotten from him since arriving in ICU. Indeed he was alive!

Olivier's healing for me in the Spirit was instant but in the natural, gradual.
As Olivier was weaned off the medicine, just as God predicted, his conscious level returned. First eye twitching and eyelids fluttering, then flailing his legs and eventually opening his eyes but he could not speak nor walk.

Mark 5:43

_____
_____
_____

The Lord had impressed upon my spirit that Olivier would be made whole in the last room he would stay in.   We were moved out of ICU, one on one care, to another section of ICU with multiple beds. Then back to High Dependency Ward where he had arrived on that first fateful night more than a week earlier. Lastly we were transferred to the 7th floor, Room 7! I was now more convinced than ever that victory was certain!

The number seven is the number of victory in the Bible. Jericho's walls came tumbling down after the Israelites had walked around the wall 7 times and gave a mighty shout! It's also the Biblical number of completion. In Genesis, after the Lord created heaven and earth, he rested on the 7th day.   I knew God would complete his work on the 7th floor in room 7 giving us a Sabbath rest.

As I reflect on my choice of food to give to Olivier after the Speech Therapist deemed him ready for a soft diet, I believe that too was Holy Spirit inspired.

Recall two things that happened to Olivier shortly after he came to live with us for the second time in Kuala Lumpur.

❖ _____

❖ _____

The waffle Olivier ate represents the wafer during communion. The water and juices symbolic of the communion wine. I mentioned to you earlier how I believe taking communion can produce a healing effect in the body. It neutralizes the illness in the body. The bread representing the broken body of Christ and the wine representing the blood shed on Calvary for our sin and sickness. We were healed by Christ's sacrifice upon Calvary's cross. No wonder after I served, 'communion' to Olivier the first time, he spoke through his own lips, *'it is done'*, and indeed it was!

Open to **John 19.30** and complete the missing scripture.

When he had received the drink, _____ With that, he bowed his head and gave up his spirit.

After I gave Olivier food he said 'It is done', in essence, it is finished!!!!!!! The next day he got up and walked! Praise the Lord!

> *Tetelestai, is only found twice in the entire New Testament, both times in John 19.*

'Got Questions.Org' says it like this:

Of the last sayings of Christ on the cross, none is more important or more poignant than, "It is finished." Found only in the Gospel of John, the Greek word translated "it is finished" is *tetelestai*, an accounting term that means "paid in full." When Jesus uttered those words, He was declaring the debt owed to His Father was wiped away completely and forever. Not that Jesus wiped away any debt that *He* owed to the Father; rather, Jesus eliminated the debt owed by mankind—the debt of sin.

Just prior to His arrest by the Romans, Jesus prayed His last public prayer, asking the Father to glorify Him, just as Jesus had glorified the Father on earth, having "finished the work you have given me to do" (John 17:4). The work Jesus was sent to do was to "seek and save that which is lost" (Luke 19:10), to provide atonement for the sins of all who would ever believe in Him (Romans 3:23-25), and to reconcile sinful men to a holy God. "All this is from God, who reconciled us to himself through Christ and gave us the ministry of reconciliation: that God was reconciling the world to himself in Christ, not counting men's sins against them. And he has committed to us the message of reconciliation" (2 Corinthians 5:18-19). None other but God in the flesh could accomplish such a task.

Also completed was the fulfillment of all Old Testament prophecies, symbols, and foreshadowing of the coming Messiah. From Genesis to Malachi, there are over 300 specific prophecies detailing the coming of the Anointed One, all fulfilled by Jesus. From the "seed" who would crush the serpent's head (Genesis 3:15), to the Suffering Servant of Isaiah 53, to the prediction of the "messenger" of the Lord (John the Baptist) who would "prepare the way" for the Messiah, all prophecies of Jesus' life, ministry, and death were fulfilled and finished at the cross.

Although the redemption of mankind is the most important finished task, many other things were finished at the cross. The sufferings Jesus endured while on the earth, and especially in His last hours, were at last over. God's will for Jesus was accomplished in His perfect obedience to the Father (John 5:30; 6:38). Most importantly, the power of sin and Satan was finished. No longer would mankind have to suffer the "flaming arrows of the evil one" (Ephesians 6:16). By raising the "shield of faith" in the One who completed the work of redemption and salvation, we can, by faith, live as new creations in Christ. Jesus' finished work on the cross was the beginning of new life for all who were once "dead in trespasses and sins" but who are now made "alive with Christ" (Ephesians 2:1, 5).

What does the Greek word 'tetelestai' mean?

How many times can you find this exact rendering in the entire Bible?   Where precisely?

In the reading above, what were some of the tasks that were *done, completed or 'tetelestai'?*

1.
2.
3.
4.
5.

Lastly my prayer had been to present Olivier to His Mom whole: God promised me he would. In both instances in 2 Kings 4:8 and 1 kings 17.22 these women received their sons back from the dead completely made whole! (Please read those stories).

Olivier's mind is intact, he's walking, talking! Whole from the crown of his head to the sole of his feet! Healed and made whole! Praise the Lord, Amen!

Take time to read the two scripture verses above. What do you think mostly links their healing to Olivier's? _____

_____

How do you think these two women felt to receive their sons back from the dead? _____

_____

How do you think my situation was similar and how do you think I felt being able to present Olivier whole to his Mom?

_____

_____

Reflection: What would you have done differently from what I did?

_____

_____

What would you have done similar? _____
_____
_____

Write what you feel is so extraordinary about Olivier's healing.

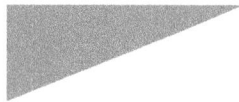

_____
_____
_____
_____

> '*For we do not want you to be ignorant, brothers of the affliction we experienced in Asia. For we were so utterly burdened beyond our strength that we despaired of life itself. Indeed, we felt that we had received the sentence of death. But that was to make us rely not on ourselves but on God who raises the dead.*'
>
> 2 Corinthians 1:8-9

Join me in giving a praise and shout out to the Lord for His wonderful works in the life of my grandson. If not for His intervention, things might have been different. Yet in His infinite grace His will prevailed in my ordeal and I believe it will in yours also! Give Him Praise!

I first heard this song in Nigeria taken from *Hannah's song* in 1 Samuel 2:2

There is none Holy as the Lord
There is none beside Him
Neither is there any rock like our God
There is none Holy as the Lord

Jehovah, you are the Most High
You are the Most, High God
The God that does what no one else can do,
How excellent is your Name,
My God You do what no one else can do,
How excellent is Your Name,
Oh Lord my God how excellent is Your Name, in all the earth, How excellent is your name!

Session 5: How I took authority over Olivier's illness and obtained his healing through faith

Week Five/ Day Four

4 Points on Olivier's Healing – Let's examine the facts

1- You must believe and not doubt: I had to get my husband Clement and Rose, Olivier's nanny to have faith and believe.
Matthew 6:5 *"When Jesus went to Nazareth he could not do many miracles there because of their unbelief. A prophet is not known in his own country. Is this not Jesus the carpenter's son?"*

2- You must have faith.
Hebrews 11:6New International Version (NIV)
"6 And without faith it is impossible to please God, because anyone who comes to him must believe that he exists and that he rewards those who earnestly seek him."

Faith of a mustard seed

"19 Then came the disciples to Jesus apart, and said, Why could not we cast him out? 20And Jesus said unto them, Because of your unbelief: for verily I say unto you, If ye have faith as a grain of mustard seed, ye shall say unto this mountain, Remove hence to yonder place; and it shall remove; and nothing shall be impossible unto you. 21 Howbeit this kind goeth not out but by prayer and fasting."

Sometimes it is necessary for you to fast to see the manifestation of healing or deliverance. Fasting allows you to have the necessary faith required to receive a miracle! When one truly fasts, your spirit man should supersede your emotional side. Your flesh should be put 'under' allowing your spirit to have dominion.

3- Jesus is willing- **Matthew 8** says a man with leprosy came down and knelt at Jesus feet and said, *'Lord if you are willing, you can make me clean'. Jesus reached out his hand and touched the man, 'I am willing (be healed,) be made clean. Jesus touched the untouchable!*

I would not entertain any thoughts from anyone who did not agree with God's Word. Neither my friends nor the doctors, nor my family. Some asked pertinent questions such as 'What if Jesus decides not to heal Olivier?' It was a logical, practical and reasonable question which I would not entertain. If I were to consider this logic it would take me out of the realm of faith and into the realm of man.

Remember, faith is now. Your thoughts must line up AND agree with God's thoughts. You cannot stand in faith yet continue to waiver in thought. The Bible says in James 1:7 a double minded person shall not expect to receive anything from God!
Besides, our God is willing to heal your sickness. The centurion had a paralyzed servant at home and told Jesus, *'I am not worthy that you come under my roof, just speak the Word and my servant will be healed.'* Matthew 8.8

4- The Word - The Word of God became my bread and water. You cannot separate God from His Word. Beloved, just one *WORD* from God is enough to turn your captivity, change your situation, heal your disease**. ONE WORD**. Expect to hear a Word from God concerning your situation.

John 1:1 says *"In the beginning was the Word and the Word was with God and the Word was God."*
I had mentioned to you my going on a fast before Easter and saying to my Bible Study ladies, I want to go on a Word fast. Be careful what you desire. At one point I wanted to trade places with my grand-son. God's Word became so real to me. As I spoke to Him, He spoke back to me through His Word.

John 15.17: reads *"if you remain in me and my Words remain in you, you can ask whatever you wish, it will be done for you."*

The Word - The Promise. This is the crux of my faith. I recounted earlier how during the second night in Singapore, Olivier's nanny arrived so I went to sleep at my friend's house. The Lord woke me up at 5:34 and as I was waiting for my friend's husband to drop me, I was talking to the Lord and he took me back to the clock's time indicating that I should read this passage of scripture:

Mark 5:34 – *"Daughter your faith has healed you, Go in peace and be freed from your suffering."*

Exercise: Take one of the 4 points mentioned above. Write the scripture and the point here.

_____

_____

Do a short one page 'dissertation' on this point using a separate sheet of paper. Look up that scripture in the Bible and read the entire story or chapter where it is found. Back up your dissertation with additional scripture gathered through research. Study how this truth can be applied in your life. Memorize the verse. Now go back to that particular point you chose and read my explanation once more. Be prepared to split up in groups in your study. Those who chose the same point, stay in one group. Explore what each has written. Debate, challenge one another. Dig deep!

Session 5: How I took authority over Olivier's illness and obtained his healing through faith

Week Five/ Day Five

How to take authority over the sickness or the issues at hand

After Jesus sent out the 72 disciples in **Luke 10**, *they saw that the demons were subject to them. Jesus commanded the disciples in verse 9 to heal the sick and tell them that the Kingdom of God has come near to you. He also told them to speak peace unto a household where they would stay. Jesus had given them authority to trample on snakes and scorpions and to overcome all the power of the enemy; nothing will harm them. Vs 19. In verse 20 the Lord told them 'do not rejoice that the spirits submit to you but rejoice that your names are written in heaven.*

Why do you think Jesus told the disciples to say the Kingdom of God has come near you?

_____

_____

How does speaking Peace to a home bring about change? _____

_____

Exercise: How to pray?

What is the most popular verse of scripture that comes to mind when you think of healing?
_____. That's right, Isaiah 53:5. You can use this verse every time to pray for manifestation of healing. Remember that healing has been accomplished by the finished work on the cross. Therefore, we need to proclaim healing and command healing according to God's Word. There are many verses out there but let's use these two today.

Write Isaiah 53:5 here_____.

Psalms 103:2-4: _____

_____

Now pray like this:

Lord Jesus, I come boldly to your throne of grace in my time of need to receive healing according your Word in Isaiah 53.5. Not only is your Word the final authority but you watch over your Word to perform it! I believe that you died for my sins and sickness and took stripes on your back for my healing. I command every organ, tissue and every cell in my body to begin to function with perfection in Jesus Name. Father, you are Jehovah Rapha – The Lord that heals me. I accept You as my healer and I confess according to Your Word in Psalms 103:2-4 that you have healed all of my diseases. Satan according to Matthew 18.18, I bind you and your cohorts from operating in my body. Spirit of infirmity (you can name it) get out of my body right now in Jesus Mighty Name. I thank you precious Jesus for your healing virtue flowing through my body renewing, restoring and revitalizing my health.

Father, let the Son of Righteousness rise now with healing in his wings over me, (my daughter, son, neighbor...) in Jesus Mighty Name I have prayed (Malachi 4:2). Amen.

In today's world it is very important to pray for safe passage when embarking on a journey. I was very proud when my son's girl-friend mentioned he prayed before the plane took off from Atlanta to Amsterdam when they came to visit! Now that is the **Covenant of Peace** in action! Recall our scripture reading from Isaiah 54:13. The Word always works!

Jesus took control of a storm and calmed the raging seas when the disciples were in a panic (Mark 4:35-44). Paul assured the captain of safe passage in Acts 27:21-26. Record what Paul said in verse in verse 22:

_____

_____

Why was Paul so certain and convinced that they would be saved? _____

_____

Not only was Paul reassured by a messenger of God, but also, God's perfect will for Paul's life was being acted out and his life had to be spared. When you are accomplishing your God given purpose, just know God is orchestrating your footsteps (Psalms 37:23) as well as all things will work out for your good (Romans 8:28).

Once I had an especially long flight from Alabama to New York and from Paris to Gabon, Africa. I had never been a stellar passenger until after this flight! From the moment we boarded, the plane took more dips and turns than Michael Jackson ever did! This lasted for almost the entirety of the flight till Paris so around 9 hours. Even the stewardesses could not serve any drinks or meals! It was really frightening.

I had begun the flight with the usual prayers but they expanded in momentum as the gravity of the flight grew apparent. I had exhausted all prayers and scriptures after more than 8 hours and finally I said something to this effect, "*So what if the plane crashes. Take my life Lord immediately so I feel no pain. I'll be in heaven anyway!*" I had to go PAST my point of fear! I had to address that fear and look at it straight in the face!

Thankfully we arrived safe and I live to tell this story. The twins were also blessed because we were on the very back row, felt the brunt of the turbulence but also was served with royalty by the stewardess' who could not serve anyone else or venture too far from their seats!

Your turn, now let's learn to pray for your own "*Travelling Graces*".

1-Protection on a plane, boat, car, train: On a plane, in order to lose the protection of the Father, let's start by first employing the Word of God. In my opinion, praying scripture is the best method of prayer. You should always find a relevant scripture to stand on. Let's read the most popular one from Psalms 91:1-2, 7:

Whoever dwells in the shelter of the Most High
  will rest in the shadow of the Almighty.[a]
² I will say of the LORD, "He is my refuge and my fortress,
  my God, in whom I trust."

Verse 7A thousand may fall at your side,
ten thousand at your right hand,
but it will not come near you.

You may also choose another scripture to stand on. This time, let's use:

Isaiah 54:17 '*no weapon forged against you will prevail, and you will refute every tongue that accuses you. This is the heritage of the servants of the LORD, and this is their vindication from me," declares the LORD.*'
You can always use scripture and personalize it when you know it is a promise to you.

Pray like this*: All things are held together by you Lord and by the Word of your power, therefore this plane is held together by your power. You have given your angels charge over me. I dwell in the shelter of the Most High and I rest under the wings of the shadow of the Almighty! My God you are my refuge ----I can hide in you. You are my strong, unshakeable fortress, I trust I am safe in you. Your Word declares that no weapon formed against me shall prevail, therefore, I take authority over terrorist attempts, bombs, stray bullets, birds flying in the engine, technical error, pilot-error--- I bind them all in the Name of Jesus.*

(Now release these things on the earth. That is your legal right. Declare some protection.)

Lord, I loose heavenly escorts to guide this plane safe to its correct destination. I (and the passengers on this plane) SHALL arrive at my (our) destination safe and sound. In Jesus Name Amen.

Always pray in the Name of Jesus. Jesus loves for you to pray in His name. In fact Jesus says, *"You can ask for anything in my name, and I will do it, so that the Son can bring glory to the Father."* John 14.13.

I will leave the last two for you to complete on your own. Some scriptures have been provided but feel free to incorporate your own or even use a different prayer point.

2- **Finances**: *You are the head and not the tail. Lender not a borrower. Blessed in the city, blessed in the country. You will lend to many nations but will not borrow from none.*
Deuteronomy 28:12, 13, Luke 6:38 *"Give, and it will be given to you. A good measure, pressed down, shaken together and running over, will be poured into your lap. For with the measure you use, it will be measured to you."*
2 Corinthians 9:8 Amplified *"And God is able to make all grace (every favor and earthly blessing) come to you in abundance, so that you may always and under all circumstances and whatever the need be self-sufficient [possessing enough to require no aid or support and furnished in abundance for every good work and charitable donation].*

Prayer:

3-**Anxiety, insomnia**: <u>**Proverbs 3:24**</u> *If you lie down, you will not be afraid; when you lie down, your sleep will be sweet. Sweet shall be your sleep and non-disturbed shall be your rest.* As we declare, angels are moving on our behalf and demons are being disarmed. Why because we have lifted our eyes to the hills and God has sent angels. When you speak a Word, heaven will help you.

<u>**Phil 4:6-7**</u> *Be anxious for nothing, but in everything by prayer and supplication, with thanksgiving, let your requests be made known to God;* [7] *and the peace of God, which surpasses all understanding, will guard your hearts and minds through Christ Jesus.*

Prayer:

Well done! That was good prayer practice which I am sure will become fluid in no time as you practice *praying right and not amiss.* You can start now making your list of prayers in your prayer journal.

Ron Carpenter says in his **ARMORED** series, we have been given the right to practice 'law' Luke <u>**10:17.**</u> The disciples were so amazed declaring to Jesus, "Even the demons are subject to us. Everybody is getting healed and delivered." Jesus said, 'I saw Satan fall like lighting. He was set over this person's house and Satan fell. Go to your neighborhood and LOOSE GOD's blessing. Behold I give you power to tread upon scorpions and serpents and nothing shall any means harm you. Be happy that your name is written in the book.

A Word of caution, just because the Word of God says you have power over scorpions and serpents, does not mean you need to go and tempt God by picking up serpents. That is not what that scripture means at all!

In Ron Carpenter's series **ARMORED,** he mentioned this very important fact: In Luke 4:1 when the devil came to tempt Jesus in the wilderness, Jesus did not dispute the authority was his. In the case of a "Will" the will is not enacted until death. But angels came and ministered to him because

Angels are Harvesters of our prayers.

Jesus quoted the Word. He said it ***It is written***. He spoke the Word. During temptation and a wilderness season, you need to speak the Word of God.

Angels came because the <u>**Word**</u> was being released although the will was not yet in effect. If you are in a wilderness and lost, you can still speak the Word in the power of the gospel.

Session 6: Release the Dove

Suggested Reading: Chapters 15-19 of Book 'Release the Dove'

Week Six/ Day One

Dove - Symbol of Peace

Dearly beloved as we end this study, we come to the crux of the matter. It's time to *Release the Dove!* For it is only when the '*Dove of the Holy Spirit*' is released into the atmosphere that truly **Healing, Blessings and Miracles** can take place.

What is the international symbol of peace? The dove with the Olive branch. I live in a nation that believe they are the "*Center for Peace*". There is a Peace Court located here in The Hague and outside, there is a "*Peace Tree*". There you can write your prayer for peace and affix it to one of the "*branches*". I have a dear friend from KL whom I fondly refer to as Lady Edwina because she is a lady in every sense of the word! She and I had the privilege of visiting the Peace Court together and placing our prayers for peace on the tree.

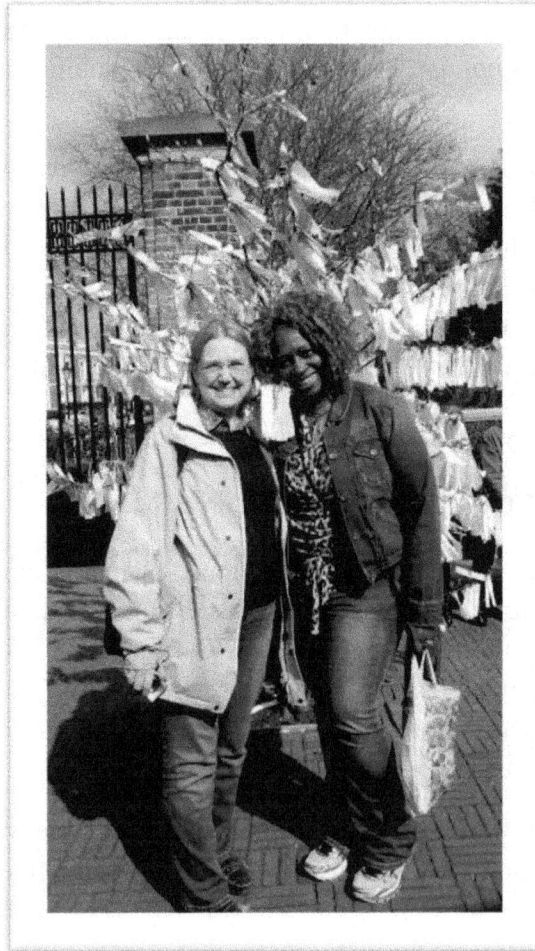

92

Open your Bibles to **Matthew 10:1-16.**

What did the Lord specifically tell the disciples to do in verse 7 of this passage? _____

_____.

According to Verse 12, what greeting did Jesus tell the disciples to give when they entered into a home? _____

The dove of the Holy Spirit has been released upon you to remain, therefore Jesus tells you to allow your peace to rest upon the home. We need to learn how to corporate with the Holy Spirit. The Spirit of God takes the simple things we do and make them effective. Dearly beloved, what divine encounters we will have if we practice this simple principle everywhere we go! If we *"Release the Dove"* in our homes, on our jobs in the marketplaces, the entire world will be healed!

Now look at the following scriptures:

Genesis 8 King James Version (KJV)

8 And God remembered Noah, and every living thing, and all the cattle that was with him in the ark: and God made a wind to pass over the earth, and the waters assuaged;

2 The fountains also of the deep and the windows of heaven were stopped, and the rain from heaven was restrained;

3 And the waters returned from off the earth continually: and after the end of the hundred and fifty days the waters were abated.

4 And the ark rested in the seventh month, on the seventeenth day of the month, upon the mountains of Ararat.

5 And the waters decreased continually until the tenth month: in the tenth month, on the first day of the month, were the tops of the mountains seen.

6 And it came to pass at the end of forty days, that Noah opened the window of the ark which he had made:

7 And he sent forth a raven, which went forth to and fro, until the waters were dried up from off the earth.

8 Also he sent forth a dove from him, to see if the waters were abated from off the face of the ground;

9 But the dove found no rest for the sole of her foot, and she returned unto him into the ark, for the waters were on the face of the whole earth: then he put forth his hand, and took her, and pulled her in unto him into the ark.

¹⁰ And he stayed yet other seven days; and again he sent forth the dove out of the ark;

¹¹ And the dove came in to him in the evening; and, lo, in her mouth was an olive leaf pluckt off: so Noah knew that the waters were abated from off the earth.

¹² And he stayed yet other seven days; and sent forth the dove; which returned not again unto him anymore.

I have studied and gleaned much from these passages, it is from here that I took Olivier's name.

Write Verse 11 here please _____

_____

_____.

In French the **meaning** of the **name Olivier** is: From the olive tree. The Dove brought back the Olive branch to signify to Noah that there was life on the face of the earth. Similarly, the '*Dove*' brought Olivier (meaning from the olive tree) back to life. Don't miss this because this might be the most important thing that you learn from this study! When you *"Release the Holy Spirit over a situation, change must take place."* God said, let there be light, and there was light. He continued to speak the world into existence and the Holy Spirit was the Engine at work!

Please write verse 8 from the reading above:

_____

_____

Noah sent the dove from himself. Please highlight that above.   From what you have learned about the meaning of the dove, what then did Noah actually send from himself?
_____. Now please think back to our discussion earlier when Jesus sent out the 72 in Luke 10:1-23. What did the Lord tell the 72 when they arrived in a home?

_____

Sisters (or brothers) in Christ, we are carriers of peace! It is the seventh verse of the Sermon on the Mount, and also seventh of what are known as the Beatitudes. In the King James Version of the Bible the text reads: "Blessed are the peacemakers: for they shall be called the children of God" (Matthew 5:9).

That's too many sevens for me indicating victory all the way! It is also important for you to know, especially us women, you can carry a sweet aroma, fragrance of peace in your home, place of business or influence and charge the atmosphere.   What is the opposite of peace?

_____.

Or you can emit a foul smelling odor.   Which one would you rather carry with you?
_____. Me too! Remember Mary who washed the feet of Jesus using expensive

nard from her Alabaster box? The perfume filled the room (Luke 7:37). Let your sweet smelling fragrance of peace and joy contaminate all who come in contact with you to the level of an epidemic!

Role play: Make up a scenario of someone bringing 'peace' in their atmosphere and someone embodying the spirit of fear and depression into their atmosphere. How do these two 'fragrant' behaviors affect the people around each carrier? In our Oasis Bible Study in KL, I would always designate Shereen to facilitate drama/ice-breakers. Everyone needs a *drama queen* in their Bible Study for this type of fun enactment.

Does it help you to 'see' this in action? _____ . If you sometimes emit the *'wrong'* aroma how might you make a change? _____

_____.

I was royally busted this week as I snapped at my son to straighten his room slash my office. Our home in Holland is cozy but the space gets cramped when there are five grown up people living under one roof for a certain length of time. With no maid service, my daughter and I have developed a working house cleaning system. Over the Christmas holidays, my son arrived and threw the house in chaos! On one of these days when I snapped at him, he had to come over to give me a hug and said *"Mom, what's going on? Surely two pieces of paper on the floor shouldn't cause you to come un-done!'*

Although an understatement of the degree of disorder present that phrase played over and over again in my head and he was right! It shouldn't. Day by day, I endeavored to incorporate small changes to avoid commenting about the house being so untidy and just learned to enjoy my son's company. The ones who live with you see the REAL you and by my son calling me on it, I was faced with a reality check so I could make the necessary changes to reflect Christ.

Your Turn

Once a friend and I were shopping at China Town in Singapore. We ran across an *"expensive Perfumerie"* and wanted to try some of their fragrances. My friend who is a *'well to do connoisseur'* of perfumes was scandalized when the seller rebuked her remark that the perfumes were fake! She was well aware of the true prices.

What would you say those living with you or those who know you best would say is the fragrance you most often embody. Be honest. If you don't know, ask them. Circle your answer.

    a) Chanel Grand Extract – $4,200 per ounce.

    b) Dolce & Gabbana - $ 50 (approximately)

c) Eau de toilette (ranges from $17 & above)

d) Cheap perfume

> One year while visiting a friend in Oman, I was blessed to purchase for my husband a set of **Amouage** cologne for men which is reputed to be the most expensive perfume in the world (my friend's sister had a friend working at **Amouage** and was able to get it at a discounted rate). Upon receiving it, my husband Clement quickly locked it up for safe keeping! Those who know him, know how funny he can be! Please *DO NOT LOCK* your scent away. Rather purpose to leave a sweet smelling aroma everywhere you go!

Spend time praying for the Holy Spirit to change your mind-set, refresh your spirit and renew your thinking to produce an agreeable perfume so that not only those around you may take notice but those in your home and are closest to you will benefit.

The song below, **Alabaster Box** by *Ceci Winans*, is sure to bless your heart. I remember when it first came out I was going through a particularly rough patch of time in my Christian Walk with the Lord. I was invited as a key-note speaker to a Women's Conference in The Hague. Although my voice was not up to par due to a cold, I endeavored to croak out my rendition of this song. Though not perfectly song, it was from my innermost being where the Holy Spirit was bringing about healing through these lyrics. Hearts were touched, I was asked to sing this song again the next day at another event.

A drama was done by our PJ Sister Church and song by "Sensational Ify" in 2015 during our *Dunamis* Women's Conference in KL (at The Ambassador's International Church). You might still be able to pull it up on Youtube.

My prayer is that you would listen to this song by *Ceci Winans*, (her melodious perfect original version) and allow the Holy Spirit to heal places in your life that are in need of repair.

"Alabaster Box"

The room grew still
As she made her way to Jesus
She stumbles through the tears that made her blind
She felt such pain
Some spoke in anger
Heard folks whisper
There's no place here for her kind
Still on she came
Through the shame that flushed her face

96

Until at last, she knelt before his feet
And though she spoke no words
Everything she said was heard
As she poured her love for the Master
From her box of alabaster

[Refrain]

And I've come to pour
My praise on Him
Like oil from Mary's alabaster box
Don't be angry if I wash his feet with my tears
And I dry them with my hair
You weren't there the night He found me
You did not feel what I felt
When he wrapped his love all around me and
You don't know the cost of the oil
In my alabaster box

I can't forget the way life used to be
I was a prisoner to the sin that had me bound
And I spent my days
Poured my life without measure
Into a little treasure box
I'd thought I'd found
Until the day when Jesus came to me
And healed my soul
With the wonder of His touch
So now I'm giving back to Him
All the praise He's worthy of
I've been forgiven
And that's why
I love Him so much

[Refrain]

And I've come to pour
My praise on Him
Like oil from Mary's alabaster box
Don't be angry if I wash his feet with my tears
And dry them with my hair (my hair)
You weren't there the night Jesus found me
You did not feel what I felt
When He wrapped his loving arms around me and
You don't know the cost of the oil
Oh, you don't know the cost of my praise
You don't know the cost of the oil
In my alabaster box

Session 6: Release the Dove

Week Six/ Day Two

Dove of the Holy Spirit

Before returning to heaven, Jesus told his disciples to remain in Jerusalem and wait for the gift the Father promised. He went on to say, John baptized with water but they would be baptized with the Holy Spirit. Acts 1: 4. In verse 8 of Acts 1, He said you will receive power

> Power is Dunamis in the Greek. Its root word is dynamite, dynamo, dynamic. It means strength, ability, power. Used 120 times in NT.

when the Holy Spirit comes on you; and you will become his witnesses. They were commissioned in Matthew 28:19-20 and in Mark 16:15. According to scripture, what was the Great Commission?

_____

_____

_____

Please list the five signs Jesus said would follow his disciples:

+ _____
+ _____
+ _____
+ _____
+ _____

The last sign is what I am mostly interested in at the moment. For it is this sign that I sought to experience in Olivier's healing. In James 5:13-14 it asks, *"Is any among you sick? Let them call the elders of the church to pray over them and anoint them with oil in the name of the Lord. And the prayer offered in faith will make the sick person well. The Lord will raise them up. If they have sinned, they will be forgiven.*

> You can make your own anointing oil or purchase from a Christian store. Directions for making your oil is found in Exodus 30:22-33

Session 6: Release the Dove

Week Six/ Day Three

What's in a name?

All the while Olivier was in hospital, I anointed him with anointing oil and laid hands on him commanding life to return. Anointing oil in the Bible was made from pressing olives. This was another way to *"Release the Dove"* over Olivier's lifeless body.

Olivier's name chosen by me and agreed to by his parents is paramount. Choosing significant names for your children is important. In the Bible, names were always given for a reason. The name you were given, you "lived out" so to speak. Jacob's name means 'holder of the heel'. He was born holding his twin brother Esau's heel, and his name is explained as **meaning** "holder of the heel" or "supplanter" (Genesis 25).

> Highly recommended, and just for fun, watch a YouTube video on how Olive Oil is pressed! Amazing!

Despite this history of ambitious trickery (thus, *"supplanter"*, one who takes the place of another), Jacob was chosen by God for greatness. Notable moments in his life include reconciling with his brother, dreaming about a stairway between heaven and earth (commonly referred to as *"Jacob's Ladder"*), wrestling with the angel of God until he received God's blessing, and receiving the new name "Israel" from the Lord, which means "contender, fighter" or *"God prevails."* Jacob was also the father of the twelve sons from whom the twelve tribes of Israel descended (**Source:** http://www.christianmeaningofnames.com/jacob/).

Or what about Sarai whose name meant ***injured princess*** but God changed it to Sarah meaning princess. Miraculously in her 90's, after being hurt in her marriage by Abraham and Hagar, she gave birth to a son, Isaac which means laughter.

Look at the story of Jabez 1 Chronicles 4:9-10, what was the meaning of his name?

_____

_____

What did he ask the Lord to do? _____

_____

How do you think Jabez changed his destiny and stood out from his brothers? _____

_____

One year, we had a wonderful woman in our Oasis Bible study by the name of Lynn Bailey who embroidered beautiful book marks with each of our names and its meaning! What a precious labor of love! May God bless you dear Lynn wherever you are!

What is the meaning of your name? For a more interesting meaning, go to:

http://www.themeaningofname.com _____

_____

_____

_____

Share with your group any insight you might have. For more fun research all your family's names, and think of a fun way to present it to them as a gift!

You may use this space:

Has your life been an epitome of the meaning of your name? _____ Have you 'lived out' its meaning? _____ Why or why not?

_____

_____Just how Jabaz cried out you too can call upon the Lord. [10] *Jabez called upon the God of Israel, saying, "Oh that you would bless me and enlarge my border, and that your hand might be with me, and that you would keep me from harm[c] so that it might not bring me pain!"* And God granted what he asked.

Oh Dear One, we can change our destinies by asking God! Jabez did! None of his brothers names are recorded in the Bible but his is! He was more honorable and sought to be a blessing and not a curse. He wanted his life to mean something, to stand for something to leave an indelible print in his generation, and it has! Many books have been written and sermons preached on these two verses! What is your heart's cry for your life beloved? What would you have God change? *Release the Dove* over it! If your life has been riddled in pain and strife and nothing has been going right, Release the Holy Spirit and watch God move!

RHONDA Name Meaning and History

What Does RHONDA Mean and History? Probably intended to mean "good spear" from Welsh rhon "spear" and da "good", but possibly influenced by the name of the Rhondda Valley in South Wales, which means "noisy". It has been in use only since the 20th century. Its use may have been partially inspired by Margaret Mackworth, Viscountess Rhondda (1883-1956), a British feminist.

Spear: a weapon with a pointed tip, typically of steel, and a long shaft, used for thrusting or throwing.

Question for anyone who knows me? Does that sound accurate?

http://www.themeaningofname.com/

Nuggets Gleaned from Today's Study:

+

+

+

Session 6: Release the Dove

Week Six/ Day Four

Dunamis Power

Back to our reading in Genesis 8:8-12. Verse 8 on page 62 says he sent out from himself a dove to see if the water had receded from the face of the earth. The dove, the peace, the Holy Spirit was sent out from himself. That is why Jesus commissioned the early disciples and has also commissioned us to release Him in our "atmosphere" to find a place for him to rest. Just today, I had an opportunity to pray for a family going through difficult times. As I released the dove over them, revelation began to flow, deliverance took place and the woman felt lighter and joyful! Now that's what happens when you take the risk to *"Release the Dove"* in your sphere of influence. You see the Holy Spirit was not given to us only to discover our identity but we are sent to invade carrying the presence of the Lord into the environment.

In John 20:19, the disciples were all together, the doors were shut, but Jesus appeared in their midst! What did he say? _____.

In verses 21-22, what did Jesus say and what did he do? _____

_____

Jesus said to the disciples, as the Father sent me, I send you. Nothing happens in the Kingdom until there is a declaration. When he breathed upon the disciples there was an impartation of the Holy Spirit. First act was to release the Spirit of God upon them. They had to find a place for the Dove to rest.

My Pastor in Alabama, Pastor Moss told me shortly before my birthday in February 2016 to *Release the Dove* in the marketplace, on my job, in my family, everywhere I was to go, I needed to Release the Spirit of God in order to change the atmosphere. To *Release the Dove* simply put, is the Great Commission we spoke of on page 97 in this work-book (Matthew 28:19-20). As a Christian, the Great Commission should be an integral part of our lives. We each have a "Greater Works Ministry" to perform for the Lord (John 14:12). When you *Release the Dove* over a situation, you Release the Holy Spirit to go forth and accomplish His purpose in the lives of the ones He indicates to you. When you don't even know *how to pray for* a situation, The Holy Spirit prays with groaning's that cannot be expressed in words (Romans 8:26). When Jesus was baptized and the Holy Spirit descended upon him like a dove, his ministry changed radically. Acts 10:38 says, *"And you know that God anointed Jesus of Nazareth with the Holy Spirit and with power. Then Jesus went around doing good and healing all who were oppressed by the devil, for God was with him. "* If Jesus had the Holy Spirit to help Him in ministry how much more you and I must have the Holy Spirit to accomplish the works of the Lord.

After speaking to my Pastor, I pondered over His Words. A few days later on my birthday I stumbled upon a pair of ceramic doves in an antique shop and purchased them. I knew this was a good omen.

As we go places atmospheres shift and change when we step into the room. The ministry of the gospel is not just in Word but in releasing the presence of God upon the earth. A few years ago we needed to have our house painted in Atlanta. I had the tedious work of collecting quotes and choosing the best man for the job. One day, my property manager and I were in the house waiting on a painter to come by, access the work and give us a quote. The gentleman walked in and we proceeded in showing him what needed to be done. All of a sudden this young man broke down into tears telling me he planned to do right by us, he said he knew I was a Godly woman because he felt *a presence in my home*. He was visibly touched. The Holy Spirit would not allow him to cheat me therefore he got the bid!

When the woman with the issue of blood touched the hem of Jesus's garment, she was made whole. The Spirit was given to Jesus without limit. The Holy Spirit was the connection between him and the Father. Jesus was immediately aware of a *release of power* when the woman touched him. There were throngs and throngs of people around him, yet he stopped and asked, "Who touched me?" Power had been released.

My dear Gem friend Carol, who rallied the Oasis ladies to pray for Olivier, offered me an extravagant gift of a drawing of the woman with the issue of blood in the aftermath of Olivier's illness. Not only did she fly the painting half way around the world, well a long way, to get to me but she personally spoke to the artist herself. So captivating is this piece of artwork that I hung it over my prayer bench. It is a constant reminder of the Lord speaking to me via my clock dial, *"Daughter your faith has healed you. Go in peace and be freed from your suffering"* (Mark 5:34).

So when was Olivier actually healed? When that Word was spoken to me. Jesus *"Released the Dove"* over me therefore, I could go into the hospital and change the atmosphere from one of mourning and sorrow to one of joy in knowing that my grandson would be made whole!

What actually does it mean to *Release the Dove*? Please indicate scripture reference.

_____

_____

According to scripture, recap what the Great Commission entails?

_____

_____

Where are we asked to be a tangible presence _____?

What did I say might be the only Bible someone reads? _____? Where
& what is the Ministry you have been called into? _____

_____

This is closely related to *Purpose*. Do you know what your purpose is? The Bible says in Ephesians 2:10: *"For we are his workmanship, created in Christ Jesus for good works, which God prepared beforehand, that we should walk in them."* Therefore Dear Ones, you were not born an accident or a mistake but God had a purpose in creating you that you must fulfill while living on planet earth. Jesus was born to die for all humanity, therefore once his purpose was up, he exited this world at 33 years old. John the Baptist, the forerunner to Christ, prepared the way for Jesus by preaching repentance and baptizing in water. When his purpose was fulfilled, he exited this world. Martin Luther King dedicated his life to the Civil Rights Movement in the 60's. He KNEW when his purpose had been accomplished and he too left fulfilled.

I think you are getting my point. Purpose is something you would do EVEN if you were not paid to do it! You no longer have permission to run helter-skelter aimlessly without purpose. If you DO NOT know what your purpose is, please take time out today to discover your God given purpose AND set a plan in motion to accomplish it! Remember Acts 10:38? The Holy Spirit will work with you to accomplish your *'ministry'*.

Notice ministry and purpose are synonymous to me. You do not need to be on a pulpit to accomplish ministry. Your purpose might be in the market-place or in a barber shop! Whatever God has given you to do, accomplish it with a *spirit of excellence*, never grumbling but do it as unto the Lord.

Please look up Colossians 3:23 and write it here _____

_____

My husband is from The Congo therefore I had moved to live there in the late 80's. I remember a period of 'ministry burnt out' which caused me to feel particularly weary. I was still in my 20's but had been heavily involved in ministry since I was 25. Learning a new language, a new culture and experiencing life had begun to show wear and tear on my body as well as my spirit. One day as I stood on the balcony of our newly built home, I prayed a breath prayer,

If a man is called to be a street sweeper, he should sweep streets even as a Michelangelo painted, or Beethoven composed music or Shakespeare wrote poetry. He should sweep streets so well that all the hosts of heaven and earth will pause to say, 'Here lived a great street sweeper who did his job well.'

-Marin Luther King Jr.

'How long Lord,'' the spirit replied immediately Hebrews 6:10. Look up the verse and write the Lord's wonderful reply to me here. _____

_____

Pastor Amos in KL often said, The **Lord is the Best Pay Master.** He was right. That's part and parcel why I sign most of my correspondence, **In His Service** *(The Lord's Service).*

Bill Johnson of Bethel Ministries said, no matter what your passion or purpose in life is, make sure you full fill the Great Commission.

The Great Commission (page 97) _____

_____

_____

My God Given Purpose (If you don't know what it is, please speak to your Bible Study Leader, Pastor or someone who knows you well. Your purpose is closely linked to your passion).
Example: *My purpose is to minister to women & to write.*

_____

_____

_____

_____

_____

_____

Above is the beautiful Art-work my Gem Friend Carol offered me. It is a magnificent piece but difficult to capture on photo. Artistic touches technique used for better viewing ONLY.

When our twins were born again at 8 years of age, so amazed were they after being filled with the Holy Spirit, they could not sleep. My son, Clement Jr., saw a vison of Jesus walking through the wall of their bedroom. It was so very surreal, yet this is the atmosphere in which the Holy Spirit operates. You see he had already commissioned the disciples. He modeled releasing his peace upon them so they would be aware of what it felt like and they could reciprocate.

Beloved, please keep in mind that these disciples had been with Jesus, watching him perform miracles, they were born again. Yet Jesus *"breathed upon th*em*"* and said, *"Receive the Holy Spirit."* This is such a controversial subject which I will not endeavor to embark upon in this study, however; it is of utmost importance that you receive the *"baptism"* (complete immersion) of the Holy Spirit, just as the disciples did, in order to do the works of Christ. This Dunamis power was different from what they received upon conversion. This was now an invading and empowering of the Holy Spirit to do the works of Christ. In John 14, this is what Jesus said,

[12] "Truly, truly, I say to you, whoever believes in me will also do the works that I do; and greater works than these will he do, because I am going to the Father. [13] Whatever you ask in my name,

this I will do, that the Father may be glorified in the Son. ¹⁴ *If you ask me[e] anything in my name, I will do it.*

You might think, do I really need the Baptism in the Holy Spirit, this is not for me? Flip back to Acts 1:5, what does it say? _____

_____.

Jesus said John baptized with water but they would be baptized with the Holy Spirit. Recall three things you learned about water baptism.

1-

2-

3-

Now, according to what you have learned about water Baptism, how would you think Holy Spirit Baptism would be similar? _____

_____

Please research the meaning of **baptizo** in the Greek. What are the synonyms used to describe baptizo:

- ✝ _____
- ✝ _____
- ✝ _____

After having properly done the research yourself, I would like for you once more to demonstrate what Holy Spirit Baptism should look like according to your research and according to what Jesus has said. Not Rhonda nor even yourself but the Word of God. In view of the photo below of water baptism, capture how the Bible says *Baptism of the Spirit* should also resemble Baptism in water. You may use the space below to record your thoughts.

_____

_____

_____

_____

_____

Baptized

for this moment

"Repent and be baptized
every one of you in the
name of Jesus Christ
for the forgiveness of
your sins, and you will receive
the gift of the Holy Spirit.
For the promise is
for you and for your children
and for all who are far off,
everyone whom the
Lord our God
calls to himself." Acts 2:38-39

Baptized
with
the
Holy
Spirit

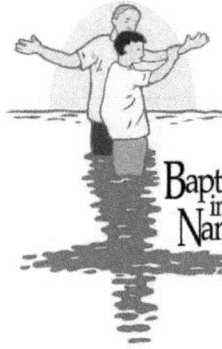

Baptized
in the
Name
of Jesus

ChurchArt Online | www.churchart.com

(Images taken from free Christian clipart)

Still not for you, I invite you to open your Bible to Acts 2:39. If you have the time, you may read all of Acts 2, it's such a glorious chapter.

"This promise is to you, and to your children, and even to the Gentiles--all who have been called by the Lord our God."

As you read, please understand that this scripture does not stand alone. You must understand it in the context in which it was given. Follow Jesus' conversation from Acts 1 to all that happened in Acts 2 to these rag tag disciples who grew from strength and power to do the works of Christ. These disciples who had gone underground, Peter had denied Jesus and all of a sudden started a public ministry after being endowed with power from on high! During Peter's first sermon, 3000 people came to Christ in one day! A transformation JUST HAD TO HAVE taken place! The dove of the Holy Spirit was released over them and they in turn *"Released the Dove"* into their environment and everywhere they went. They were persecuted but they continued the work set before them.

Bill Johnson of Bethel Ministries said, *"Peter realized what he had. He said to the lame man what I have, I give unto you, Rise up and walk! People brought the sick out along the road when Peter went to pray and people where healed from his shadow! Shadows have no substance. They have no power. What overshadows you will shadow you."* Simply amazing!

He goes on to say, *"A depressed Christian will not walk into a room and see people healed. When you are depressed you are turned inward. You become a dead sea. Nothing goes out and nothing comes in. You are wrapped in anxiety. Do not be preoccupied in your inadequacies but in who He is. Never give people what you have to offer. Instead give them Jesus."* Priceless!

He concludes, *"There was such a presence over Paul the tent-maker that they took aprons he worked in and people were healed. It was upon him to alter and change the environment around him. When I am turned inward, I'm restricted to allow the Holy Spirit to flow. Paul says you are restricted by your anxiety. Jesus healed touched and delivered so many people in 3 ½ years that the earth could not contain all of the testimonies if books were written. That is the Holy Spirit and its presence on one person. So significant that Peter learned how to host the presence of the Holy Spirit and allow the dove to abide on him.*

The Spirit of God is in us but there is a presence that is there according to the assignment and 'yieldedness' we have. Paul was a tent maker so powerful that his anointing could heal the demon possessed. Peter did not lay hands (on people) it was just the presence of God."

Exercise: Please place a T next to the statement you feel is True, place an F next to the one which is false. An explanation where requested.

1- Peter was a Tent-maker _____.

2- Peter's shadow healed people _____.

3- According to Bill Johnson, a depressed person can heal the sick_____. Why or why not?

_____.

4- Peter denied Jesus three times_____.

5- I cannot heal a person unless I am anointed with the Holy Spirit_____. Why or why not?

_____

I believe "*Release the Dove*" book and workbook are a mandate from God. I went on a year's Sabbatical and in that period of time concentrated a few months on completing this mandate. After, Olivier's illness, many Oasis sisters asked just how I was able to endure such a horrific experience and emerge completely unscathed. Here in this book and work-book I am unloading ALL the goods necessary to do the works of Christ and see the miraculous.

One thing that I did during Olivier's convalescence was to pray without ceasing. I was able to accomplish this by praying in the Spirit.

"Likewise the Spirit helps us in our weakness. For we do not know what to pray for as we ought, but the Spirit himself intercedes for us with groaning too deep for words" (Romans 8:26).

"Pray in the Spirit at all times, with every kind of prayer and petition. To this end, stay alert with all perseverance in your prayers for all the saints" (Ephesians 6:18).

If you are able to pray in tongues, take time out today to pray for a particular situation. Allow the Holy Spirit to pray in your stead. Record thoughts here.

_____

_____

_____

_____

Nuggets Gleaned from Today's Study:

+

+

+

DIGGING DEEPER TREASURE HUNT. So indented into my innermost being is that Word from Mark 5:34. A miniature study will give you further insight in putting the *"Act"* of the woman with the issue of blood into perspective. Seeing this *"Act"* through Jewish eyes is crucial. I invite you along on this journey on a dusty road in Jerusalem. Come with me and the woman with the issue whom I will refer to as **Faith**, as she grabbed hold of Jesus' tassels, and was made completely whole! Beloved, I too had the privilege of being in the throngs, watching the Master perform miracles and when it was my time to touch the hem of His garment, armed with the knowledge that it was He who bade me come, I went!

FAITH TALKS

"18Against all hope, Abraham in hope believed and so became the father of many nations, just as he had been told, "So shall your offspring be." 19Without weakening in his faith, acknowledged the decrepitness of his body (since he was about a hundred years old) and the lifelessness Sarah's womb 20Yet he did not waver through disbelief in the promise of God, but was strengthened in his faith and gave glory to God," Romans 4:18-20

18Against all hope, **RHONDA** in hope believed and so became the **Grandmother** of many nations, just as **she** had been told, "So shall your offspring be." 19Without weakening IN HER faith, acknowledged the decrepitness of his body (since Olivier was on life support and paralyzed without a good medical prognosis) 20Yet **SHE** did not waver through disbelief in the promise of God, but was strengthened in **HER** faith and gave glory to God..

YOUR TURN

18Against all hope, _____ in hope believed and so became the _____ of many nations, just as _____ had been told, "So shall your offspring be." 19Without weakening _____ faith, _____acknowledged the decrepitness _____ (SINCE _____)

_____ 20 Yet _____ did not waver through disbelief in the promise of God, but was strengthened in _____ faith and gave glory to God...

OK! Let's dig in………………………

Tassels *(Ref. this section:* https://therefinersfire.org/tallit.htm)

In Matthew 9:20-22, we find a curious story of a sick woman receiving healing simply by touching Jesus' clothes: *"Just then a woman, who had been subject to bleeding for twelve years, came up behind Him and touched the hem of His garment; for she said to herself, 'If I only touch His cloak, I will be healed.' Jesus (Yeshua) turned and saw her. 'Take heart, daughter,' He said, 'your faith has healed you.' And the woman was healed from that moment."* In the Mark account of the same story, it continues:

"At once Yeshua realized that power had gone out from Him. He turned around in the crowd and asked, 'Who touched My clothes?' 'You see the people crowding against You,' His disciples answered, 'and yet You can ask, Who touched Me?'" (Mk. 5:30-31).

What is so significant about the hem of Jesus' garment? At first reading, it seems an odd practice. However, once we understand the significance of the hem of one's garment, these passages will have much more meaning. The word translated, hem, is actually referring to the fringes, or tassels (called tzitziyot, in Hebrew), required to be on the four corners of all clothing of Jewish men, in accordance with God's instruction:

"The Lord said to Moses, 'Speak to the Israelites and say to them: Throughout the generations to come, you are to make tassels on the corners of one's garments, with a blue cord on each tassel. You will have these tassels to look at and so will remember all the commands of the Lord, that you may obey them and not prostitute yourselves by going after the lusts of your own hearts and eyes. Then you will remember to obey all My commands, and will be consecrated to your God. I am the Lord your God'" (Numbers 15:37-41).

In ancient Israel, men wore four-cornered outer tunics with these tassels, or tzitziyot, tied to the four corners. This outer garment became known as a tallit, and eventually evolved into the more formal prayer shawl. But, why tassels? These tassels were to remind each Jewish man of his responsibility to fulfill God's commandments. In fact, these tassels are tied into 613 knots to constantly remind them of the 613 laws of Moses, of which there are 365 prohibitions (The "thou shalt not" laws), and 248 affirmations (the "thou shall" laws). The knots also correspond with the ineffable name of God, the unspoken yod-hey-vav-hey, Yahweh.

Because they were hanging on the four corners of your garment, in full view of everyone including yourself, they would be a constant reminder to walk according to God's Laws. The Hebrew word we translate as Law, is halacha, and it literally means "walk." You see, following God's law is a daily walk and stay on his path of righteousness, we all need constant reminding.

Wearing these tassels would be comparable to us wearing a large Bible on a rope around our necks. How would we behave in public, how would we speak to others, where would we go? God intended them to be a constant reminder of His Word when he told the Israelites to wear these fringes. Today, because Jewish people wear western clothes, they keep this law by wearing a four-cornered garment as an undershirt. Yet, they bring the tassels out over their belt so that they can be seen. We also find the tzitziyot on the corners of the beautiful prayer shawls worn by Jewish men as an outer garment when they pray.

When deep in prayer, Jewish men will put these prayer shawls over their heads to shut out the world and be in the presence of God. This can be seen in the synagogue or at the Western Wall in Jerusalem. The prayer shawls are white, representing the heavens, or the dwelling place of the Lord. And, the color blue represents the Ruach HaKodesh, or Holy Spirit of God. Therefore, praying under the tallit, or prayer shawl, is covering yourself with the presence of God. From biblical times, this custom was like a prayer closet, and it is likely this is what Yeshua was referring to in Matthew 6:6, when He told us to get into our closet, apart from the people around, and pray in secret to the Lord.

This tallit was the mantle worn by Samuel (I Sam. 15:27), and it was Elijah's mantle that was conferred upon Elisha (I Kgs. 19:19). It was also worn by Yeshua, and the "hem of the garment" that was touched by the woman with the issue of blood was actually the tzitziyot or tassels of His tallit. Even in His glorious Second Coming, Yeshua will be wearing His tallit. In Revelation 19:11-16, John gives us a description: "*I saw heaven standing open and there before me was a white horse, whose rider is Faithful and True, He has a name written on Him that no one but He Himself knows. He is clothed in a garment dipped in blood: and His Name is The Word of God... On His garment and on His thigh He has a name written: King of Kings, and Lord of Lords*" (Rev. 19:11-13, 16). J. R. Church suggests that the vesture is the tallit of Yeshua with His titles written upon it and on His thighs. Where do the tzitziyot fall, but on one's thigh? Notice there are four titles listed in this passage - perhaps one for each of the four tzitziyot:

"*A Name written, that no man knew but He Himself*" - the ineffable name of God, Yahweh! (v. 12); "*The Word of God*" (v. 13); "*King of Kings*" and, "*Lord of Lords*" (v. 16).

The purpose of the four fringes on a garment was, and is, and still will be to proclaim the Word of the Lord, so as to remember them and perform them.

WORK IT OUT

From the above reading, flesh out five things that you found very enlightening. Discuss with your small group.

1

2

3

4

5

Authority

These tassels also came to be associated with a person's authority. Saul and David: In the case of King Saul, we find that David humiliated him by sneaking up to him in a cave at the Spring of Ein Gedi and cutting off Saul's tassels, a symbol of his authority.

Boaz and Ruth: Another example of the authority represented in the tassel is found in a passage in the book of Ruth, which is sometimes difficult to understand. In Chapter three, Ruth went to Boaz to receive his blessing that would help her out of her difficult situation. She went to the threshing floor and slept at his feet.

"In the middle of the night something startled the man, and he turned and discovered a woman lying at his feet. 'Who are you?' he asked. 'I am your servant, Ruth,' she said. 'Spread the corner of your garment over me, since you are a kinsman redeemer'" (Ruth 3:8-9).

He immediately understood and said to her: "Don't be afraid. I will do for you all you ask. All my fellow townsmen know that you are a woman of noble character" (Ruth 3:11). He proceeded to make every arrangement to help her, and eventually, he married her. What Ruth did in asking Boaz to spread the corner of his garment over her was a symbolic way of saying she was placing herself under Boaz's authority.

Under his wings

❖ Find the account in your Bible regarding David and Saul. 2 pts! Next, why do you think David did not annihilate his enemy Saul at that time?

❖ Look ahead to find out how Saul and Jonathan were killed and what was the penalty to the bearer of "good" news? Why do you think David did that to him? 2 pts!

❖ What is the "Tassel of Authority that you carry as a believer?" Please note scripture reference.

Let's go back to the woman on the shores of the Sea of Galilee who came to Jesus for healing. When she pressed through the crowd, she was not content to just pat Jesus on the back. She was a desperate woman, who had spent all of her money on cures that did not work. It was a bold step for her to push through that crowd of people, for according to Levitical law, it was forbidden for her to be out in public with her condition, for she was considered unclean (Lev. 15:25). However, she was at the end of her rope. She had nothing to lose. She had heard of the Messiah who could heal and she anxiously sought Him out. But why did she want to touch the hem of His garment - the tassels of His tallit?

These *tzitziyot* were a point of contact she needed to help her release her faith to receive a miracle in her life. What did they represent? First, they represented the Word of God, which is always the place where we can find healing for all the needs in our life. Second, the fringes also represented the authority of Yeshua. She had heard that many people were healed by Yeshua, that He taught with authority, and when He spoke, people were healed.

Third, there was even more to these fringes. The prophet Malachi spoke of the Messiah of Israel and said of Him, *"But for you who revere My name, the sun of righteousness will rise with healing in His wings"* (Mal. 4:2). The Hebrew word for "wings" used in this passage is kanaf, which is a word that specifically means the fringe-like feathers or edges of a bird's wing, not the whole wing. All of us have seen an eagle or hawk circling in the summer sky and have seen these fringe-like feathers. This word, therefore, had two meanings and could be translated wings, or fringes.

The woman had heard Yeshua was the Messiah. Perhaps she remembered this messianic promise from the scroll of Malachi and thought, if I am to be healed, then will it be found in His wings... His *tzitziyot*? By faith, she reached out and touched the fringes, and was healed.

It is interesting that all though the Old Testament, the Hebrew word for wings in most passages is *kanaf* when referring to God. Surely, the place of refuge is under the kanaf of the Lord, i.e., under His Word and His authority! In a different passage, some time later Yeshua arrived at the town of Genessaret, also on the shores of the Sea of Galilee. The men of the town recognized Yeshua and sent word out so that many people brought all their sick to Him and begged Him to let the sick just touch the fringe of His garment. The Bible simply reports, "All who touched Him were healed" (Mk. 6:53-56). These people were not healed simply by touching the fringes of Yeshua's garment in a crowd. They were healed when their faith touched the power of God and the One who could heal their infirmities. It was their point of contact to release their faith to receive a touch from the Lord.

The bottom line is, while we no longer have "four cornered garments" today, the command to wear tzit-tzits was never removed! Some say "the Holy Spirit" replaced the command.

What about you and me? None of us is without a need in our life, whether it be healing, family problems, financial or emotional problems. Do we have the simple faith to reach out and touch the hem of the garment of Yeshua? If you do, He is waiting to meet our needs, even today.
(Reference above Jewish Reading: JR Church Teachings).

WORK IT OUT

1 These *tzitziyot* were_____

2- According to Levitical law, it was forbidden _____.
What were some of the risks/ _____?

3- _____ (wings) specifically means the fringe-like feathers or edges of a bird's wing,
not the whole wing.

Look at these Word Treasures.

How can you relate them to the idea of the "Sun of righteousness"? _____
_____

Do you remember the name for God our Righteousness in the Greek? _____

What do you recall about the God of Righteousness and YOUR stance in God? _____
_____

Matthew 23:37

*36Truly I tell you, all these things will come upon this generation. 37 O
Jerusalem, Jerusalem, who kills theprophets and stones those sent to her, how often I have
longed to gather your children together, as a hen gathers her chicks under her wings, but you
were unwilling! 38Look, your house is left to you desolate....*

Ruth 2:12

*"May the LORD reward your work, and your wages be full from the LORD, the God of Israel,
under whose wings you have come to seek refuge."*

Session 6: Release the Dove

Suggested Reading – Postlude, Praise Report, Final Reflections

Week Six/ Five

Final Reflections

In this last session Day 5, I will address the Final Reflections written on pages 96-98 of *Release the Dove Book.* Please complete the reading before attempting to answer these questions. I will refer to the Final Reflections writer as Madame Shola Adeyemi Bero.

Questions

1- In paragraph 3, Madame Shola Adeyemi Bero says 'that those who live in the Spirit must also strive to always walk in the Spirit for it is only by walking in the Spirit we find peace that surpasses all understanding and solutions that bring *rest.'* Beautiful statement, but how can one find peace and rest in a time of crisis? Provide scripture reference.

_____

_____

2- In paragraph 4, Madame Shola Adeyemi Bero said, Kuala Lumper was life in the letter, while Singapore represented life in the Spirit. Please read 2 Corinthians 3:3-6 and tell why you think that is so:

_____

_____

3- In paragraph 5, according to Madame Shola Adeyemi Bero, what messages does the dove bring? _____

_____

4. In paragraph 5, the dove came back with an olive leaf which signified _____.

5. On page 65, we looked at meanings of names. Go to the website provided and write out the information you find on Olivier's name. _____

_____

6. In paragraph 6, Madame Shola Adeyemi Bero says 'with the power of the Word, water and waffles did the trick.' What else have I mentioned that waffles and water were symbolic of?

_____

7. On page 95, paragraph 5, Olivier echoed the Words of Jesus when He said, 'It is finished'. Explain what Jesus meant when He said, 'It is finished'. I encourage you to back up your argument with scripture. _____

8. Why do you think those where the first words out of Olivier's mouth after his ordeal in ICU? _____What do you think would have been more appropriate for a 9 year old? _____Could this be another way of God using the simple things to confound the wise? _____

9. On the last page, 98 of Release the Dove Book, the Elijah anointing is mentioned, what is the Elijah anointing and who was he in the Bible? Research may be necessary.

_____

_____

10. Dearly Beloved, we are at the end of my particular story, where does yours begin? If you want to become a bonafide "*Releaser of the Dove*", walking in the supernatural miracle worker, then there are steps you must take that might just defy the ordinary. What is the miraculous anyway? What is a miracle?

A Biblical miracle in google dictionary is described as an extraordinary and welcome event that is not explicable by natural or scientific laws and is therefore attributed to a divine agency. A remarkable event or development that brings very welcome consequences. For example:

"The miracle of Jesus rising from the grave".

"Jesus first miracle was to turn water into wine."

Synonyms: supernatural phenomenon, mystery, prodigy, sign

From these definitions and synonyms, write what you believe a miracle to be.

_____

_____

Depending on YOUR definition and YOUR belief of a miracle is the deciding factor whether or not you will see the miraculous take place in your life.

Recall the Biblical meaning of Faith including Bible reference_____

_____

Now what ISN'T Faith? _____

Our popular go to phrase '*seeing is believing*' DOES not apply to Faith, at least *NOT* in the natural.

Let's get real here, if you are willing to watch all of the Sci-Fi movies that are on the market, watch scary movies, go to a fortune teller, do your horoscope ......if you believe in that side of the world's belief of the supernatural, why can't you believe in the Biblical Supernatural view?

It is *NOT* one and the same by any means, I simply wanted to draw your attention to the things we do in society without batting an eye yet when it comes to the supernatural things of God, our eyebrow is raised with that extra dab of eye-liner and mascara!

The wisest man who has ever lived, King Solomon said that there is nothing new under the sun (Ecclesiastes 1:9) and he is very correct! You might argue what about all the new technology in the world today. Well, who says that doesn't exist in another realm? Remember the piece on Abraham I had you read back in Chapter 2 of this workbook? I can see some of your thoughts racing a mile a minute wanting to discuss *"the existence of UFO's or how the pyramids were created,"* or some other strange phenomenon but *NO dear-heart*, let's not go there. Please let's stay within context.

I am speaking of Biblical miracles which are listed in both the Old and New Testaments. Let's bring things closer to home, this is about you. In the grand scope of things, when you are getting up to have that first cup of coffee and sit down to read your emails just to find out your brother has been in a car accident and is now in ICU, what would be your first reaction? That is what I want to illicit from you today. Kingdom reactions and Kingdom thinking. When Oasis Leading Ladies Barb and Loma were at my home on that fateful Thursday in March 2015, before I changed Olivier's doctor, mundane things were taking place. Although Olivier had been ill for nearly six days at that point, I did not freak out but in my initial state, I did not forget to pray. As soon as our meeting was over and both Barb and Loma had prayed for Olivier's recovery, I left for the hospital expecting a miracle diagnosis and I got one FINALLY!

The other day, I was speaking to Carol, my Gem Friend, on the miraculous. As I had penned an email to her a day earlier, the Lord had impressed upon my spirit the word 'bath-tub". Now, Carol had just celebrated a birthday so all kinds of thoughts were running rampant through my mind but I had to obey the spirit. When Carol phoned and we got over our pleasantries, she asked what I meant by the bathtub. Of course I had NO idea and explained to her what I just explained to you. She proceeded in saying that in the house they just moved to in Houston her bath-room is very unusual and especially the tub because over it there are infrared healing lamps! You could have knocked me over with a feather! I could not have known that but the Holy Spirit did! Carol and I had been praying about a specific healing issue and the Lord had given me scripture but he had also provided something quite ordinary in which to receive healing. Here in Holland, many people use infrared healing lamps for healing of depression especially during our long harsh winters with little day-light. We even have them in my Health Club!

The point that I am trying to make is this: The miraculous is usually accompanied by having to do something "seemingly foolish". Have you heard of Naaman in the Bible? Let's cast our final launch into the deep before bringing this study to a close. If you've never heard of Naaman, get ready to be sufficiently amused.

Please open your Bibles to the delightful story of Naaman found in 2 Kings 5. After reading chapter 5, answer these questions below.

1-Who was Naaman?

2-What was his issue?

3-Who offered a solution?

4-To which land did he need to go to obtain a cure?

5-What did the King of Israel do when he read Naaman's letter?

6-Who came to his rescue?

7-What did the prophet tell him to do? Do you recall what number 7 is symbolic of?

8-What was Naaman's reaction?

9- Who persuaded Naaman to do as the prophet proposed?

10-What was the result of Naaman's obedience?

In both instances of persuading Naaman to do something to receive his healing, who were involved?

   a. Doctors
   b. Chiropractor
   c. Homeopathic individuals
   d. Servants

I certainly hope you circled d! The little slave girl and Naaman's servants were all considered "insignificant" people yet it was through them that this VIP received his miracle. Please tuck that fact a way for future reference.

I'm chuckling just imaging what you must be thinking as you read this story for the first time. The reason for my exercise above was for you to have a clear cut view of what Naaman's problem was and how it was solved miraculously. On any given day, you might go and have a swim and *Not* be cured of your ailment. What was so different about Naaman's case? _____. I would like you to probe and dig deeper. Write out verse 8 here _____

_____

_____

Cross reference that with 2 Chronicles 20:20 _____

_____

No matter which version you read, the statement ends with 'so shall you prosper or succeed'. Would you say that Naaman's expedition was a successful one and why or why not?

Would you say that Elisha was rather pompous, why or not? Before you respond, carefully consider verses 15 & 16 in 2 Kings 5. What do you think was most likely Elisha's reason for his words of surety to Naaman? _____

Spend a few minutes fleshing out this very rich story with your Bible mates before turning the bend towards our finish line.

In the days of the prophets, the Word of God came through the man of God. Believers had the law and the temple but they looked to a prophet to hear from God.

When Jesus was baptized, the Holy Spirit descended upon Him in the embodiment form of a dove. *"16 And when Jesus was baptized, immediately he went up from the water, and behold, the heavens were opened to him,[c] and he saw the Spirit of God descending like a dove and coming to rest on him; 17 and behold, a voice from heaven said, "This is my beloved Son,[d] with whom I am well pleased."* Matthew 3:16 NIV.

The Holy Spirit "rested" upon Jesus. The Holy Spirit needs to rest upon each of us to accomplish the works of God. Don't miss the next thing that happens: Immediately afterwards, the Holy Spirit led Jesus into the wilderness to be tempted by the devil! There he fasted for 40 days and for 40 nights.

What is your 'wilderness' or your God given purpose to fulfill on planet earth? Beloved brace yourself, YOU WILL BE TEMPTED. You will be tempted in the WORD OF GOD. Jesus was tempted. In your trials, tribulations or ministry, expect to be tempted. That is a part of the package of being a Christian. The devil will always say as He did with Adam and Eve, "Did God REALLY SAY?" He will test you on God's Word. He will twist God's Word to cause you to doubt the Lord. It was that way in the beginning and it is the same today. Jesus was tested on God's Word, therefore you are not excluded.

The Holy Spirit was released upon the earth to do the works of God only after Jesus was crucified and resurrected. He ascended unto the Father leaving the Holy Spirit to help us fulfill our purpose on earth in our daily lives and to accomplish the miraculous.

There was a period of time when the Word of God was rare in 1 Samuel 3:1

The boy Samuel ministered before the LORD under Eli. In those days the Word of the LORD was rare; there were not many visions.
There was a time in history when the Lord was silent. These were the 400 years between the Old and the New Testament. I would not have wanted to live in either of those eras. Then with the coming of Jesus Christ, the silence was broken.

"But when the set time had fully come, God sent his Son, born of a woman, born under the law." Galatians 4.4.

I cannot ignore the fact that I'm wrapping up this work-book during a most historical event in history of our nation, the election of America's 45th President. This election has caused even more scandal than the previous. There has been more separation of families and groups of people than I have seen in my entire life. Yet, I am assured of the providence of God.

I send forth **The Dove of Peace** to fly over our nation. It is amazing how God utilizes history to work out his purposes. Though it might appear as if we are living again in the days that might be termed "the silence of God," when for almost 2,000 years there has been no inspired voice from God, we must look back and just as God was at work during those 400 years, He is at work now! Everything He needs to say has been said in the Old and New Testaments. *"In the fullness of time"* our Lord will bring everything to pass as he said He would, so Dear-heart, let *not* your heart be troubled. Just as God was quietly making preparations for the babe Christ to come, don't you think preparations are being made for His return!

Today we have more means of spreading the gospel than ever before, we have more missionaries, and more Christian channels, more Christian books and DVD's, virtually everything needed to deliver the gospel to those who need it. Yet we still seem to experience such desolation in our own lives. What is needed is for us to take a stand and release the dove of peace in our own atmospheres.

God's purposes have not ended, for sure. He is working them out as fully now as he did in those days. Just as the world had come to a place of hopelessness then, and the One who would fulfill all their hopes came into their midst, so the world again is facing a time when despair is spreading widely across the earth. Hopelessness is rampant everywhere and in this time God is moving to bring to fulfillment all the prophetic words concerning the coming of his Son again into the world to establish his kingdom. How soon will Jesus appear? God knows. But what God has done in history, he will do again as we approach the end of *"the silence of God."*

(Ref above: https://soundfaith.com/sermons/36132-400-years-of-silence-short-vesion)

Let us pray:

*"Our Father, our faith remains rooted and grounded in your Word and not just historical things. Although it is integrally related to life we pray that our own faith may grow strong and be powerful as we see the despair around us, the shaking of foundations, the changing of that which has long been taken to be permanent, the overthrowing of empires and the rising of others. Abba, our eyes are steadfast on you as our Unchanging Omnipresent God. The One Whose Word is Eternal. As the Lord Jesus himself said, "Heaven and earth shall pass away, but my Word shall never pass away." Matthew 24:35. (Lift up your hands as a sign of surrender unto God) Use me oh Lord in this latter day to become a catalyst for change. In my sphere of influence enable me to **Release the Dove** and see miraculous occurrences take place. I pray in Jesus Mighty name, Amen.*

If you prayed that prayer with a sincere heart, get ready for a supernatural manifestation to take place!

Remember one of our key scriptures read,

'Very truly I tell you, whoever believes in me will do the works I have been doing, and they will do even greater things than these, because I am going to the Father.' John 14.12

Let's make that our last memory verse to learn.

Dear Ones, I hope that I have successfully demonstrated that it is only with the enabling of the Holy Spirit that we can have faith to experience the miraculous in our lives. Thanks for coming alongside me on this Glamma's journey of faith. My sincere hope and desire is that you will take these truths and apply to your daily lives. I would like to challenge you to start to '*Release the Dove*' in your atmosphere of influence, right here and right now!

My next book will be a ***Release the Dove*** devotional designed to help each reader remain in the flow of faith and the miraculous on a daily basis!

In His Service,

Koko

I would love to hear your stories, please write me at RD534@outlook.com

MY SELECTION OF SONGS

Word of God speak by Mercy Me

I'm finding myself at a loss for words
And the funny thing is it's okay
The last thing I need is to be heard
But to hear what You would say

Word of God speak
Would you pour down like rain
Washing my eyes to see
Your majesty
To be still and know
That you're in this place
Please let me stay and rest
In your holiness
Word of God speak

I'm finding myself in the midst of You
Beyond the noise
All that I need, is to be with you
And in the quiet, hear your voice

I'm finding myself at a loss for words and the funny thing is, it's ok.

How Great is our God by ChrisTomlin

The splendor of the King, clothed in majesty
Let all the earth rejoice
All the earth rejoice

He wraps himself in Light, and darkness
tries to hide
And trembles at His voice
Trembles at His voice

How great is our God, sing with me
How great is our God, and all will see
How great, how great is our God

Age to age He stands
And time is in His hands

Beginning and the end
Beginning and the end

The Godhead Three in One
Father Spirit Son
The Lion and the Lamb
The Lion and the Lamb

Name above all names
Worthy of our praise
My heart will sing
How great is our God

How great is our God, sing with me
How great is our God, and all will see
How great, how great is our God

BE MAGNIFIED, by Don Moen

I have made you too small, in my eyes
O Lord, forgive me
And I've believed in a lie
That you were unable to help me.
But now O Lord, I see my wrong
Heal my heart and show yourself strong
And in my eyes,and with my song
O Lord, be magnified
O Lord, be magnified.

Chorus
Be magnified O Lord,
You are highly exalted
And there is nothing you can't do
O Lord, my eyes are on you, be magnified,
O lord be magnified Lord be magnified
verse 2
I have leaned on the wisdom of men
O Lord, forgive me

Thy Will by, Hilary Scott

I'm so confused
I know I heard you loud and clear
So, I followed through
Somehow I ended up here
I don't wanna think
I may never understand
That my broken heart is a part of your plan
When I try to pray
All I've got is hurt and these four words

Thy will be done
Thy will be done
Thy will be done

<u>Imela , Imela Eze m oh (Thank You! Thank You My King)</u>
<u>By Nathaniel Bassey & Enitan Adaba</u>

Verse 1
When I think upon your goodness;
And your faithfulness each day
I'm convinced it's not because I'm worthy-
To receive the kind of love that You give.
But I'm grateful for your mercy,
And I'm grateful for your grace
And because of how You've poured out Yourself,
I have come to sing this song out in praise

Imela, Imela (Thank You! Thank You!)
Okaka, Onyekeruwa (Great and Mighty Creater of the world)
Imela, Imela, (Thank You! Thank You!)

Eze m Oh (My King)

Verse 2
Who am I to sing Your praises?
Who am I to worship You?

And make a way to enter into Your throne
I could not come near Your presence
I could never sing Your song
But the sacrifice on Calvary's tree
Is the reason I can cry out today

Refrain
Onyedikagi? Ekene diri gi (Who is like You? Al Glory belongs to You)
Onyene mema (He who does good)
Onyedikagi? Ekene diri gi (Who is like You? Al Glory belongs to You)
Onye nagworia (Mighty Healer)
(Repeat)

REDEEMER, Written by Nicole Mullen

Who taught the sun where to stand in the morning?
And who told the ocean you can only come this far?
And who showed the moon where to hide 'til evening?
Whose words alone can catch a falling star?

Well, I know my Redeemer lives
I know my Redeemer lives
All of creation testifies
This life within me cries
I know my Redeemer lives, yeah

The very same God that spins things in orbit
Runs to the weary, the worn and the weak
And the same gentle hands that hold me when I'm broken
They conquered death to bring me victory

Now I know my Redeemer lives
I know my Redeemer lives
Let all creation testify
Let this life within me cry
I know my Redeemer, He lives

To take away my shame
And He lives forever, I'll proclaim
That the payment for my sin
Was the precious life He gave
But now He's alive and there's an empty grave

And I know my Redeemer, He lives
I know my Redeemer lives
Let all creation testify
Let this life within me cry
I know my Redeemer

I know my Redeemer lives
I know my Redeemer lives

I know that, I know that, I know that, I know that
I know my Redeemer lives
Because He lives I can face tomorrow

I know, I know, He lives, He lives, yeah, yeah
I spoke with Him this morning
He lives, He lives, the tomb is empty
He lives, He lives, I've gotta tell everybody, yeah

128

Good, Good Father, by Chris Tomlin

Oh, I've heard a thousand stories
Of what they think You're like
But I've heard the tender whisper
Of love in the dead of night
And You tell me that You're pleased
And that I'm never alone

You're a good good Father
It's who You are, it's who You are, it's who You are
And I'm loved by you
It's who I am, it's who I am, it's who I am

Oh, and I've seen many searching
For answers far and wide
But I know we're all searching
For answers only you provide
'Cause You know just what we need
Before we say a word

You're a good good Father
It's who You are, it's who you are, it's who you are
And I'm loved by you
It's who I am, it's who I am, it's who I am

Cause You are perfect in all of your ways
You are perfect in all of your ways
You are perfect in all of your ways to us

You…

How Great is our God, Chris Tomlin

The splendor of a King, clothed in majesty
Let all the earth rejoice
All the earth rejoice

He wraps himself in Light, and darkness tries to hide
And trembles at His voice
Trembles at His voice

How great is our God, sing with me
How great is our God, and all will see
How great, how great is our God

Age to age, He stands
And time is in His hands
Beginning and the end
Beginning and the end

The Godhead, Three in One
Father, Spirit, Son
The Lion and the Lamb
The Lion and the Lamb

Name above all names
Worthy of all praise
My heart will sing
How great is our God

How great.....

Jesus, we enthrone You, by Don Moen

Jesus, we enthrone You
We proclaim You, our King
Standing here, in the midst of Us
We raise You Up with our praise

And as we worship, build a throne
And as we worship, build a throne
And as we worship, build a throne
Come, Lord Jesus, and take Your place

Jesus, we enthrone You
We proclaim You are King
Standing here, in the midst of Us
We raise You Up with our praise

And as we worship, build a throne
And as we worship, build a throne
And as we worship, build a throne
Come, Lord Jesus, and take Your place

And as we worship, build a throne
And as we worship, build a throne
And as we worship, build a throne
Come, Lord Jesus, and take Your place.

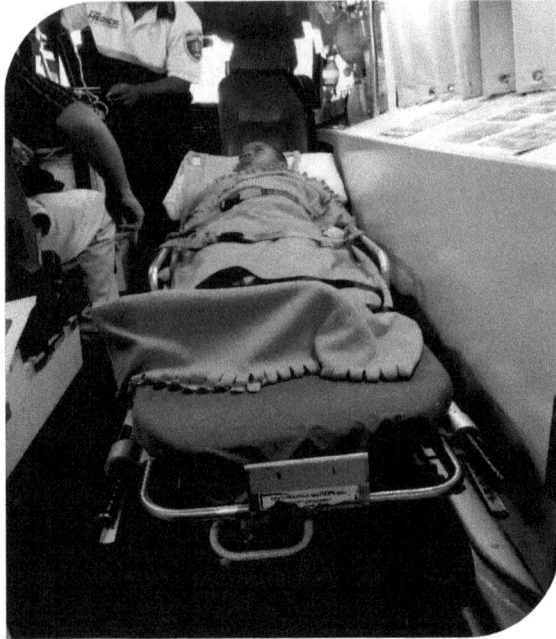

Left: Day Evacuated from KL to Singapore. Below Left: Me laying hands on Olivier speaking to his eyes to see, ears to hear and mouth to speak (Ezekiel 37). Below Right: The day Olivier opened his eyes

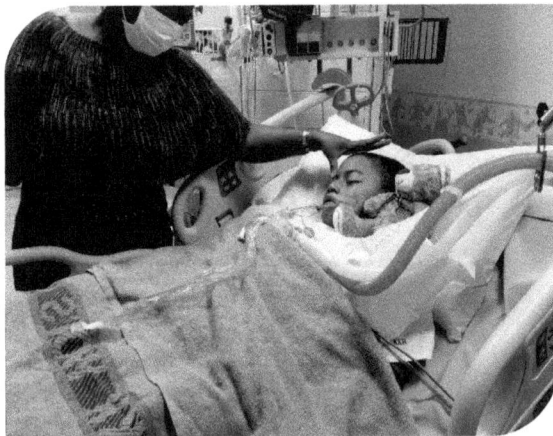

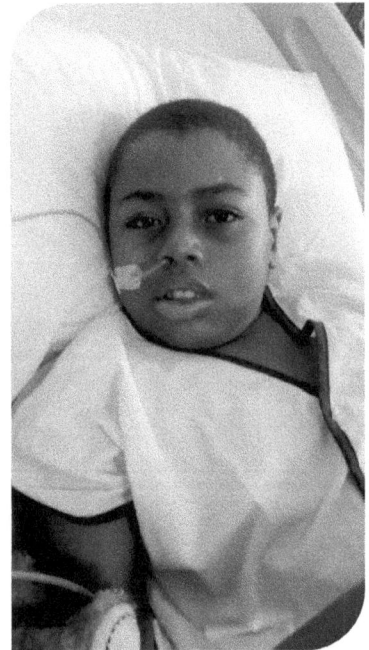

First Publication January 2017

ISBN-13: 978-1-78222-515-7

www.ingramcontent.com/pod-product-compliance
Lightning Source LLC
Chambersburg PA
CBHW081602040426

42452CB00013B/2491